Expecting First Time Moms

The Complete Day by Day Pregnancy Guide on What You Should Expect for a Healthy First Year, Motherhood, Childbirth, and Newborn from Leading Experts who Are Parents too

Emily Green

© Copyright 2019 - All rights reserved.

The content contained within this book may not be reproduced, duplicated or transmitted without direct written permission from the author or the publisher.

Under no circumstances will any blame or legal responsibility be held against the publisher, or author, for any damages, reparation, or monetary loss due to the information contained within this book. Either directly or indirectly.

Legal Notice:
This book is copyright protected. This book is only for personal use. You cannot amend, distribute, sell, use, quote or paraphrase any part, or the content within this book, without the consent of the author or publisher.

Disclaimer Notice:

Please note the information contained within this document is for educational and entertainment purposes only. All effort has been executed to present accurate, up to date, and reliable, complete information. No warranties of any kind are declared or implied. Readers acknowledge that the author is not engaging in the rendering of legal, financial, medical or professional advice. The content within this book has been derived from various sources. Please consult a licensed professional before attempting any techniques outlined in this book.

By reading this document, the reader agrees that under no circumstances is the author responsible for any losses, direct or indirect, which are incurred as a result of the use of information contained within this document, including, but not limited to, — errors, omissions, or inaccuracies.

Contents

Chapter 1:
The Start of Your 9-Month Journey ----------------------------------- 1

Chapter 2:
Selecting Your OB/GYN --- 9

Chapter 3:
The Morning Sickness Remedy ------------------------------- 19

Chapter 4:
Exercising Do's and Don'ts --------------------------------- 29

Chapter 5:
Sleeping the Right Way -------------------------------------- 36

Chapter 6:
Nutrition and Top Foods to Eat ---------------------------- 44

Chapter 7:
Tips to Curb Cravings --------------------------------------- 53

Chapter 8:
The First Trimester, Weeks 1 to 12 ------------------------- 59

Chapter 9:
The Second Trimester, Weeks 13 to 26 ---------------------------- 65

Chapter 10:
The Third Trimester, Weeks 27 to 40 ---------------------------- 71

Chapter 11:
The Stages of Labor -- 79

Chapter 12:
Hypnobirthing -- 88

Chapter 13:
Post-partum Recovery -- 97

Chapter 14:
Detrimental Mistakes to Avoid During Pregnancy ----------------- 107

Chapter 15:
Top Pregnancy Tips and Essentials ------------------------------ 118

EXPECTING FIRST TIME MOMS

The Complete Day by Day Pregnancy Guide on What You Should Expect for A Healthy First Year, Motherhood, Childbirth, And Newborn from Leading Experts Who Are Parents Too

---

Emily Green

Chapter 1:
The Start of Your 9-Month Journey

It has been said there are events in a lifetime that are so significant that they leave a distinct 'before' and 'after' in your life and in you as a person. The day you find out that you are expecting your first child is one such event. The feelings that a woman experiences when that pregnancy test turns positive can only be felt and understood by the woman herself. In the case of an unexpected pregnancy, there might be shock and panic. In the case of a long-awaited child, joy and happiness can be overwhelming and leave you in tears. Apprehension, anxiety, and fear are some of the other feelings a woman might experience after finding out that they are going to be a mother. After these emotions settle, you are likely going to experience an overwhelming urge to start planning. Some women will start buying baby clothes immediately after finding out that they are pregnant.

Usually, a woman suspects that they are pregnant even before they take that pregnancy test. This suspicion could be because of the way they feel or because of the circumstances of the previous weeks. The best way to be sure is to take a pregnancy test. A positive pregnancy test can be confirmed at the hospital, at which point you'll know for sure that there's no turning back. Questioning whether you're up to the task of being a mother is a common and natural emotion to experience after finding out that you are pregnant. Are you ready? Is your partner ready? Is your career ready? These are just some everyday worries that women go through. It is essential that you prioritize having a safe and healthy pregnancy above anything else that can be handled later.

There is no 'perfect' approach to pregnancy, but there are certain guidelines that are generally accepted as requirements for a healthy pregnancy and childbirth. For starters, after finding out that you are pregnant, you'll need to kick all your bad habits to the curb. Smoking and excessive consumption of alcohol are two examples of things you'll need to forget. Some things that are not exactly textbook-bad will need to go too. For instance, if you have previously enjoyed sushi, you'll have to make do without it for the next nine months. If you enjoyed contact sports before you got pregnant, you might want to settle for yoga instead. If you were a fan of long, hot baths, you might need to settle for showers instead. In short, pregnancy will change your life. You must be ready for these changes.

Being ready will incorporate the physical and the mental. It is often said that your attitude can change the course of your life, and this is true for pregnancy. A positive attitude during pregnancy will make this journey more enjoyable and memorable for the right reasons. Thanks to all the hormonal changes that occur during pregnancy, you're likely to experience mild to severe mood swings which can throw quite the spanner into the works. Stay conscious of your emotions and keep a positive mindset. Meditation, taking a relaxing bath, having an honest, open conversation with a confidant, and therapy can help you manage all the differing emotions that you'll experience during this period. Staying mentally and physically healthy during pregnancy will increase your chances of remaining healthy and happy after becoming a mom.

Just like some girls plan their dream wedding well in advance, some moms plan their kids' births even before they get pregnant. Whether you're the type that likes to start early or the kind that prefers to arrive late, it is important that you at least have a rough plan in mind. Over the coming months, you can refine your plan to include more details. A significant decision you'll need to make is whether you wish to have a home birth or hospital birth. If you wish to have a home birth, you'll need to choose a good midwife and a doula who will assist you with the delivery.

A midwife is a health care provider who can deliver babies, while a doula is more of a professional support system for you. A doula will teach you how to manage the pain of childbirth including guiding you on breathing techniques. A good midwife and a good doula are vital assets to have during delivery. On the flipside, if you opt to go to the hospital, you'll need to start looking for a good hospital and preferably one that accepts your insurance plan, if you have one. It is important to note that a midwife can also help you deliver at a hospital.

Throughout the next nine months, your baby will grow from the size of an orange seed to the size of a small pumpkin or watermelon. You will experience hormonal, physical, and emotional changes as your baby grows. Some of these changes will be wonderful, and others will be unpleasant. Keeping your eye on the goal will take you through the most challenging days. Learning how to manage the manageable changes will come in handy — worried about stretch marks? Get yourself a sweet moisturizing cream like cocoa buttercream to keep your skin soft and stretchy, so it's not pulled too tight. Take care of your skin by paying attention to what you put inside of your body. Fruits like oranges that are packed with vitamin C are recommended. Some things will be mostly outside of your control as far as managing them goes. Are you worried about gaining weight? You do not have a whole lot of choice in this when you are growing a baby inside of you. You need to ensure that you're eating the right things.

Your womanhood should not take a backseat during pregnancy. Pregnancy is a time to celebrate not just the baby inside of you but you as a woman as well. A lot of times, pregnant women forget to take care of themselves and focus a lot on nurturing the pregnancy. It is advisable and vital that you make time to do the things you enjoy as a woman and as a person. This self-care should continue even after the baby arrives. Pamper yourself by going for pedicures and manicures and allow others to pamper you when they want to. As far as going to the spa is concerned, check with your doctor first as specific spa treatments could harm your baby. For instance, it is generally advised to hold off massages and intensive facials until you're into your second trimester. Saunas are a no-no for the entire duration of your pregnancy, as they can cause overheating which is dangerous to the baby.

Dental care is another form of self-care that you'll need to observe during your pregnancy. You might probably have heard it said that dentists are not too keen to offer dental treatments to pregnant women. This is not entirely true. Dental work that is necessary and urgent such as treatment of a cavity can be carried out during pregnancy. For dental work that is mainly aesthetic, such as teeth whitening, it is usually best to wait until after delivery. While pregnant, your dentist will use the minimum dose of anesthesia and will likely recommend that you visit during your second trimester. In your third trimester, you are likely to be very uncomfortable lying on your back in the dentist's chair.

A good health insurance plan will alleviate your financial worries during your pregnancy. Good healthcare is not exactly cheap and knowing that your insurance provider is carrying the more massive load of the financial burden will mean one less problem on your plate. Ideally, it is best to get on an insurance plan before you get pregnant. If you were not on an insurance cover before you got pregnant, you could still get the coverage you need for your maternity needs. Being uninsured could cost you tens of thousands of dollars over the next nine months, so it's always advisable to get on board an insurance cover.

While most women are more than willing to share the good news of their pregnancy with their loved ones, the tune changes when it comes to facing the employer. It can be challenging to break the news of your pregnancy to your boss, especially when you are apprehensive about how your maternity break will affect your career aspirations. It is good practice to let your employer know you are expecting and will be away from work before they find out for themselves. Sharing this information early on allows your employer enough time to plan for your absence, especially if they need to hire a replacement to hold the fort when you're away. Feel free to wait until you're twenty weeks along to break the news to your employer. Since your bump starts showing between weeks 12 and 16, you'll need to make sure nosy co-workers do not get to the boss before you. Layering and keeping the information to yourself until you are ready to let it be public knowledge should help. What this means is that you'll not announce anything on Facebook until you're prepared for everyone to know.

The people who love you are a priceless asset for you during pregnancy. They'll come through for you in ways you had never imagined. They'll cry tears of joy with you when you find out that you are pregnant. They'll plan your surprise baby shower for you and buy too many clothes for your baby. They'll hold your hair as you throw up during the first trimester and stay awake with you when you cannot sleep during the third trimester. Cherish these people and let them know how much they mean to you. It is easy to be a mean and terrible person when you are dealing with all the pregnancy hormones but do your best to resist the urge. Your partner may not understand how frustrating it is to get up a million times a night to pee, but they are also dealing with this life event as well. They're probably worried about what kind of father they'll be and if they'll live up to expectations. Be mindful of this and keep having the conversations that matter.

Encourage your partner to be a part of your pregnancy by signing up for childbirth education classes together. Your partner will come in handy during delivery when they are reciting to you all the useful tips that they learned during that Lamaze class. Often, it is easy for a father-to-be to feel left out from the pregnancy journey since the pregnancy is such an intimate time for baby and mom to bond. Going for classes, engaging in fun activities together, and reminding yourself why you got together in the first place is essential in telling your partner that you still need them, and they still matter to you. Make sure to schedule as many date nights as you can, since they'll probably become a thing of the past after the baby comes home.

Emily Green

Pregnancy is a delicate period, and you need to be aware of warning signs that indicate that you need to get to the hospital. Things that could previously be ignored might need to be checked during pregnancy — having a suspicious rash down there? Get it checked. Are you feeling abnormally nauseous in the mornings? See a doctor. Are you worried that you have a urinary tract infection? Book that doctor's appointment. Do not self-medicate, especially not during pregnancy. Self-medication is the surest way to harm yourself and your baby.

Lastly, enjoy your pregnancy. It is a beautiful journey that will last only nine months, and once it's over, all you will have left are memories. Living each day at a time, while making the most of it, is the perfect way of going through the three trimesters. Accepting that you do not need to have everything figured out will give you peace of mind. The Universe chose you to be your baby's mother, and that is your sign that you are good enough for this most fulfilling job.

Chapter 2:
Selecting Your OB/GYN

After finding out that you are pregnant, you'll have to say goodbye to your general practitioner and say hello to a new kind of doctor: the obstetrician. An obstetrician is a doctor who specializes in obstetrics, which is the field concerned with all matter's pregnancy and childbirth. An obstetrician differs from a gynecologist in that gynecology focuses on the female reproductive systems without necessarily venturing into the childbirth and pregnancy process. In simple terms, your regular gynecologist might not be suited for your pregnancy unless they are an obstetrician as well.

As a first-time mother, it is crucial to choose an obstetrician who makes your pregnancy journey easier. A knowledgeable, experienced, and caring OB/GYN can help you navigate a pregnancy smoothly by offering the right professional guidance. In the event of a high-risk pregnancy, an obstetrician can ensure that all precautions are taken to guarantee the comfort and safety of mother and baby. This nine-month companion will play a significant role in ensuring the well-being of yourself and the bundle of joy growing inside of you.

Emily Green

Some women will already have a preferred doctor way before they get pregnant. This is ideal and allows you to get started on the pregnancy journey with the right medical partner. If you haven't already chosen an obstetrician, it is not too late. You can still look for a great OB/GYN after you're already pregnant. Allow yourself enough time to look for the right doctor. Do not rush the process as this could negatively affect your pregnancy and birthing experience.

An excellent place to start looking is by asking your general physician or gynecologist for a recommendation. Ask them why they think the OB/GYN they are recommending would be a good match for you. An objective peer review will help you decide based on facts and not camaraderie.

Your family and friends are another resource you'll want to use for referrals. It's highly likely that a few births have happened within your social circle. Ask about those. Talk to your friends about their birthing experiences. Reach out to your aunties for referrals. If several people mention a specific doctor, investigate that one. They might be the right doctor for you.

You'll also want to leverage the power of social media and other online sites for your benefit. Thankfully, it has become relatively easy to find information online. Do your research and find out what people have to say about an OB/GYN. Reviews on social media sites and online forums should be taken into consideration. Remember, one bad review might be an outlier. However, if everyone seems to have had a bad experience with a certain OB/GYN, yours will not be any different.

When selecting an obstetrician, you'll need to consider your preferences. For instance, some women feel more comfortable having female doctors. Others might prefer male doctors. Start by deciding which gender you are most comfortable with. Professional experience and qualifications should always take precedence over gender.

If you wish to avoid out of pocket costs, go for obstetricians that are recommended through your insurance coverage. Your insurance provider will provide a list of physicians and hospitals covered by your plan. If you do not already have this list, you can request one. This list will also help you choose a doctor who has access to your preferred hospital if you already have one. If you are not tied down by the restrictions of an insurer, you have more leeway when it comes to choosing hospitals and doctors especially if you have an unlimited budget.

Consider the accessibility of the obstetrician, in terms of physical distance and after-hours policy. You'll want to choose a doctor you can easily reach should you need to. You really do not want to be driving for hours to get to your OB/GYN's office, as this could be extremely exhausting especially in the last weeks of your pregnancy. As far as after-hours are concerned, choose an OB/GYN who is available to take care of you in times of emergencies. Emergencies do not always wait for working hours, and you need someone you can always reach.

At the very least, choose an obstetrician who has a back-up plan if they are unreachable. If you opt for a group practice, ensure you are aware of who should take over when your usual OB/GYN is away. If it is a private practice, ask about the arrangements that have been made to take care of patients when the sole doctor is not on call.

Consider making a list of three doctors who meet your preliminary criteria (whatever this might be) and arrange for a meeting with each of them. This meeting will be your chance to ask important questions and determine if you are comfortable around them. Remember, a doctor might be highly experienced and still not be a good fit for you. For your pregnancy and birthing experience, you need someone with whom you fit well, someone that you are genuinely and wholesomely comfortable around, as there will be lots of bare-naked truths to share during this journey.

Some of the questions you can ask during the first meet and greet session with your obstetrician include:

- How many years have you practiced as an OB/GYN?

- How many births have you attended?

Expecting First Time Moms

- Which hospitals do you have access to?

- If I choose you, where would I deliver?

- Would you be available for the delivery, or would I be handed over to another doctor? Why?

- How many babies do you deliver every month?

- How many patients do you see per day? How long is each appointment?

- What are your views on the various birthing preferences and how do you accommodate your patients' preferences?

- Have you had any experience with high-risk pregnancies?

- How many C-sections have you performed? How many C-sections do you perform in a month?

After asking each of these questions to your list of three possibilities, now ask yourself some questions as well:

- Did you like the doctor's communication style?

- How was their bedside manner?

- Did the rest of the staff seem helpful and friendly?

- How was the office? Was it clean?

- Is the office conveniently located?

- Did you have to wait long to be seen?

With these questions answered, you can now settle on the doctor that you feel is right for you and get started on your prenatal visits.

Your prenatal appointments should ideally begin at eight weeks of pregnancy. Your first prenatal visit will typically be the longest. This is the familiarization meeting where your doctor gets to find out everything, they need to know about you. It is vital that you arrive ready to answer all the questions that the doctor might have. These will include questions on your medical history (including family medical history), birth control methods, last menstrual period, medications you're taking and/or allergic to, among others.

During your first visit, your obstetrician will also conduct an array of tests. These include a Pap smear test and several blood tests. These tests will be performed to ascertain your health status, for your benefit and that of your child. The blood tests, for instance, will be done to determine your HIV status, hemoglobin levels, blood type, Rhesus factor, sickle cell status, and even your Rubella status.

It is critical that you are entirely truthful with the doctor during the first visit (and the subsequent ones as well) as this will give them a full understanding of you and your medical history. Prenatal visits are neither the time nor the place for bashfulness. Be open with the obstetrician, answer questions, and volunteer any helpful information that you might have. The more information the doctor has on you, the better they can help you. If you are unsure about anything (for instance, your family's medical history), say so. Don't make things up for the sake of answering. You might be putting yourself and the baby at risk.

Based on the outcome of your laboratory tests and the consultation, you should expect to get some guidelines from your doctor regarding:

- Allergies, medications, dental care, diet, and environmental hazards
- Travel and physical (exercise, sex) limitations, if any
- Prenatal vitamins and supplements
- Miscarriage precautions

Before leaving your obstetrician's office, make sure to ask whom to call in case of an emergency. You should also get clarification on what constitutes an emergency. This will also be your chance to get a schedule in place so that you know when you are expected to be at your obstetrician's office throughout the next nine months.

Usually, a healthy pregnancy will require fewer visits during the early stages and progress to more frequent visits as you approach the delivery date. A typical schedule for a healthy pregnancy will involve one prenatal visit a month from week four to week 28, one prenatal visit every two weeks from week 28 to week 36, and finally, one prenatal visit per week from week 36 to week 40 and beyond.

Certain risk factors will necessitate deviating from the typical schedule. These include being thirty-five years and older and/or having preexisting health problems. Medical problems that arise during the pregnancy, for example, preeclampsia, will also require that you visit your obstetrician more often for closer monitoring.

After your first prenatal visit, your subsequent visits will be pretty much similar. They will involve your doctor monitoring your blood pressure, weight gain, the baby's growth, and heart rate. Your doctor will also keep an eye on your hands and feet to check for swelling. Later, as the pregnancy advances, your doctor will recommend ultrasounds at appropriate times to check for any birth defects and even to check the gender if you wish to find out. The ultrasound to check gender might be repeated later for confirmation, especially if the baby's positioning left some room for doubt.

Some of your prenatal visits will also require that you undergo special tests to check for gestational diabetes and other conditions. This is more so if you have a history of certain medical conditions in your family. It is also during the prenatal visits that you'll receive any vaccines that you'll require. An example of a vaccine that you'll be offered is the whooping cough vaccine, which you will get between weeks 27 and 36. These vaccines are administered to protect you and your unborn baby.

You can keep a notebook in which you'll record any questions you need to share with your doctor during your visits. Pregnancy brain (the forgetfulness that comes with pregnancy) is a thing you might struggle with. Your notebook will come in handy in ensuring you do not forget any important things that you might want to consult with your doctor on.

First-time moms will usually be excited to get started on their prenatal visits as soon as possible. However, before eight weeks, there's not much to be done during a prenatal visit. During the first one to eight weeks after conception, the most an obstetrician can offer is a confirmation of pregnancy and maybe a general health check. This should put you at ease because it means you have at least eight weeks to grab yourself Dr. Right if you do not have one already.

The exception to the rule is if you have had any health complications or consider yourself a high-risk pregnancy. In this case, you should get yourself to an obstetrician soonest possible after the home pregnancy test turns positive. This will ensure that you get the medical attention you require immediately to alleviate any risks to you and the unborn baby. If you have been taking any long-term medication, you'll also want to consult with a doctor immediately after finding out that you are pregnant. This is because some medicines can be harmful to the baby, and you'll need to know what your options are as far as managing your condition vis-à-vis ensuring baby's safety.

If you already have preferences in terms of how you intend to approach your birth, you need not be tied down by that when choosing an obstetrician. Most medical professionals are ready and willing to accommodate the views and preferences of expecting moms. You only need to have an open discussion where you let your doctor know how to envision your birth to be like. For instance, your perfect doctor does not need to be a hypnobirthing expert just because you are interested in hypnobirthing. You can make it work either way.

Choosing an obstetrician who is a good fit for you the first time helps you have an easier time with your subsequent births should you choose to have multiple children. Women who use the same obstetrician for their multiple children have an easier time during prenatal visits as they do not have to explain their medical history all over again. They also settle into an easy, solid, and comfortable relationship with their doctor, a fact that can be very reassuring to an expecting mom.

Chapter 3:
The Morning Sickness Remedy

Nausea and vomiting are two of the earliest signs of pregnancy. Unfortunately, for some women, these two unwelcome guests make themselves comfortable well into the pregnancy, sometimes continuing into the second and third trimester. Morning sickness is the term that is used to refer to nausea and queasiness that occurs when a woman is expecting a child. This nausea comes about because of the sudden increase of hormones in the body. This dramatic shift in the hormones is beneficial to the development of the unborn baby. It is a different ballgame for the expecting mother.

Morning sickness is named so because the symptoms are likely to manifest during the early hours of the day. For many women, this is the case. It is necessary to note that morning sickness can happen at any time of the day and night.

When it does happen, morning sickness can take away the joy from a pregnancy. It is uncomfortable and has been known to impact a woman's appetite negatively. It cannot be very comforting to know that anything you eat will be thrown up a few hours later. If you are experiencing morning sickness, you can take specific steps to feel a little better. You might be unable to rid yourself of nausea and vomiting completely, but you can take small steps to alleviate the severity of either or both.

The first thing you'll want to do is take a good look at your diet and find out if you're eating anything that might trigger morning sickness. Common culprits include caffeine, spicy foods, and fatty foods. If you have always enjoyed your cup of coffee, it might be time to switch to something milder like tea. Toss the fast food and opt for some blander alternatives that are high in proteins and carbs. Some women report being triggered by seafood so you might want to check how you're reacting to this as well. The trick is to avoid any foods that are overwhelming in terms of flavor and aroma, as these have a high potential to cause morning sickness.

In their absence, you'll want to ensure your diet remains balanced and somewhat enjoyable, for your sake and the baby's as well. Go for foods that are mild flavored but rich in nutrients. These include cooked vegetables such as carrots or squash and fruits. Carbohydrates such as rice and baked potatoes are also nourishing and do not trigger morning sickness. You'll also want to keep some ginger nearby if you are struggling with morning sickness. Ginger has been shown to alleviate morning sickness, and you can have it in your tea or even bake some ginger cookies to snack on during the day.

Expecting First Time Moms

As mentioned earlier, when morning sickness moves in, your appetite might move out. While you might not feel like eating, it is critical that you do. Your body needs the nourishment, and most importantly, your baby needs it too. The trick is to ensure that you eat small meals spaced throughout the day. Instead of having three large meals, have several small meals and snacks throughout the day. Drinking enough fluids throughout the day also helps. As with the food, ensure this is taken in small quantities as getting too full on fluids or food will make you feel queasy. Your body will be more receptive to cold liquids so ensure you put some ice in your drinks and take small sips throughout the day.

Tiredness will make your morning sickness worse, so ensure you get plenty of rest at night and even during the day. Schedule naps during the day, take breaks when you need to, and get to bed on time. While your body is changing and the baby inside of you is growing, you will be using up lots of energy. Resting ensures that you replenish your energy supply. In the morning when you wake up, do so slowly. Getting up and out of bed suddenly can trigger nausea.

As far as triggering nausea, exhaustion goes hand in hand with stress. When pregnant, it is essential to avoid stress as this hurts you and the baby. If you're struggling with morning sickness, stress is an even greater enemy. Stress hormones will only make the symptoms of your morning sickness worse. There are various ways of combating stress. One is to avoid stressful situations and environments. The other is to calm your mind using tried and tested means such as meditation and relaxation exercises. Chamomile tea is also a great relaxer and will send you straight to sleep.

Besides your diet and lifestyle, other factors could contribute to your morning sickness. Strong perfumes and fragrances, for instance, can trigger queasiness. If you seem to feel particularly nauseous in the bathroom, consider replacing all the scented soaps and shampoos with unscented products. Forego your powerful deodorant and stay away from the body splashes for a while.

Most women will have morning sickness only for the first trimester, after which the symptoms go away. For other women, morning sickness lasts throughout the pregnancy. As an expecting mom, it is vital that you're aware of the differences between morning sickness and another more severe condition known as hyperemesis gravidarum.

Hyperemesis Gravidarum

Hyperemesis gravidarum, abbreviated as HG, is the more severe cousin of morning sickness. It is a pregnancy complication that occurs in some women and can have dire consequences if not treated. If you suspect that you have HG, you should head to a hospital immediately for medical attention. Failure to do so can lead to severe dehydration which is harmful to you and your baby.

If you experience any of the following signs and symptoms, you might be suffering from hyperemesis gravidarum:

- Nausea that is always accompanied by severe vomiting
- Nausea that does not subside or go away as the pregnancy progresses
- Severe dehydration
- Inability to keep any food down
- Extreme fatigue
- Jaundice
- Low blood pressure
- Increased heart rate
- Headaches and confusion

Depending on the type of hyperemesis gravidarum that you have, you could either get medication or be hospitalized. Mild cases will require you to take certain meds and observe dietary and lifestyle changes. For severe cases, a hospital stay will be necessary so that you can receive fluid and nutrition through an intravenous line (IV).

Some women will get relief from hyperemesis gravidarum as their pregnancy progress. For others, this complication will require management throughout the pregnancy. If you fall into this category, there are several treatment options available to you to make you as comfortable as possible. One of these is acupressure.

Acupressure focuses on the pressure point that reduces nausea, thus stimulating the body to heal itself by applying the right kind of pressure through massage. Some women will opt for acupuncture, which is often more effective than acupressure when it comes to activating the body's healing ability. Both acupressure and acupuncture are ideal treatment options as they are not detrimental to the mom or baby.

It is important to note that morning sickness differs from woman to woman and from pregnancy to pregnancy. As such, while you might have an easy first pregnancy with little to no morning sickness symptoms, this could change with your second baby. The solution is to be alert to your triggers, and then make the necessary changes that will ensure you get as comfortable as possible during your pregnancy journey. In case of uncertainty, always consult. As with the prenatal visits, keep a notebook if you must. Writing down when you felt most nauseous can help you identify patterns. You can after that use this information to come up with lasting solutions, including determining the foods that seem to trigger your nausea.

Quick Snacks for When You Have Morning Sickness
When you're dealing with morning sickness, sometimes all you'll want are practical recipes that you can quickly whip together. Morning

sickness will not be such a drag when you know you can kick it to the curb with a five-minute recipe. Consider preparing any of the following snacks when you cannot seem to keep anything down:

Ginger Cookies

Ginger cookies can be quickly baked at home using carefully measured portions of all-purpose flour and ground ginger. You can also add other spices such as cinnamon and cloves, but only if they do not make your nausea worse. If you are not up to the task of baking, you can stock up on store-bought ginger cookies, at least until you're able to bake.

Lemonade

Many pregnant women find that lemonade settles their queasy stomachs, so try making some at home. Home-made lemonade is much better than store-bought as you can control the amount of sugar that goes in. You can also substitute sugar with a healthier alternative like honey. Not only is lemonade great for making you feel less nauseous, but it's also packed with vitamin C, which is an antioxidant. Coupled with some ice cubes, a glass of lemonade will help you feel refreshed and settled in no time.

Coconut Water Smoothie

When going through morning sickness, you'll likely be getting dehydrated from losing so much water. Coconut water is precisely what the doctor recommends as far as keeping you hydrated. Not only is it naturally hydrating and so sweet to the taste, but it also contains five electrolytes that are needed by the body. These are sodium, magnesium, potassium, phosphorus, and calcium. The body needs these electrolytes for the healthy function of cells, nerves, and tissues.

To make coconut water even more interesting, make a smoothie with bananas and strawberries. Make sure the strawberries to clean the berries thoroughly as you do not want to introduce pathogens in your body. Bananas are rich in several vitamins and minerals including potassium and vitamin B6 while strawberries are an excellent source of vitamin C.

Vegetable Soup
You can make an easy vegetable soup using readily available vegetables such as cauliflower and zucchini. If you like, throw in some celery and carrots as well. To avoid making the soup too bland, throw in some seasoning like garlic, bay leaf, and even oregano. Vegetable soups are nourishing and gentle on your sensitive stomach, which is precisely the sort of balance you need in your life right now.

Banana-Oat Muffins
You can never go wrong with bananas and whole oats. These are easy to prepare, and you can make a batch of them to last you the entire week. For best results, use wholegrain rice flour. Wheat flour can easily irritate some people's stomachs, and you do not want to be taking chances when you're pregnant.

Easy Fix Fruit Salad

If you're only able to keep down fruit, make sure it is good fruit. While you cannot survive on fruits alone, sometimes, all you need is a refreshing bowl of fresh fruit salad. The best fruits to eat during pregnancy, especially when facing morning sickness, are those that are refreshing and packed with vitamins. Watermelon, for instance, is packed with vitamins A and C, iron, and calcium. Watermelon is 90% water, which means it is also highly hydrating. Other fruits that you should include in your salad include oranges, mangoes, avocados, bananas, and apricots. A fruit salad is a good snack to carry to work with you as it is easy to make in the mornings and doesn't spoil easily when stored well.

Chicken Salad

A chicken salad is easy to prepare and makes for a good snack or even a whole meal depending on the portion. To make chicken salad, you'll need a baked chicken that has been cut into small pieces. You'll also need mayonnaise, celery, lemon juice, and pepper. If you like, you can add grapes and almonds as well. Chicken salad is a wonderful recipe in that it is something that you and your partner can have for dinner without getting worried about monotony. You'll only need to make sure that you switch up the ingredients and you'll be good to go.

Quinoa Salad

Quinoa is a superfood that contains proteins, iron, all nine essential amino acids, and B vitamins. It makes for an excellent source of nutrients during pregnancy. To make a quinoa salad, cook quinoa first in a saucepan of boiling water. It takes about ten to fifteen minutes for quinoa to cook well. Once done, strain and rinse with cold water, making sure that all moisture has been removed. Transfer the dry quinoa to a salad bowl and toss in whatever you wish. This could be onion, tomato, olive oil, pepper, and parsley. The best thing about this salad is that you can have it as many times as you like without compromising on your nutritional requirements.

Greek Yogurt Snacks

Greek yogurt is rich in protein and highly nourishing. When pregnant, it is recommended that you give more priority to Greek yogurt, if you can, as you'll get more nutrients this way. To make Greek yogurt interesting, consider using it as the replacement for certain items in your everyday meals. For instance, use Greek yogurt as a salad dressing, or as a replacement for sour cream in quesadillas. Adding Greek yogurt to pancake mix makes your pancakes filling and wholesome, especially if you opt for wholegrain flour.

Chapter 4:
Exercising Do's and Don'ts

After finding out that you are pregnant, you'll probably start to wonder where certain things fit in your life. Take exercise for instance. If you were highly active before pregnancy, you'd likely be wondering whether you need to slow down or even just quit. As a rule of thumb, exercise is recommended during pregnancy. Exercise is beneficial to pregnant women in various ways. For starters, exercise releases endorphins which are the hormones responsible for making you feel happy and relaxed. It's common for pregnant women to suffer mood swings during pregnancy, and the feel-good hormones throw a delicate balance to the mix. Exercise during pregnancy helps to ease some of the physical discomfort experienced by expecting moms by stretching your muscles and preventing cramping. Staying active is also a great way to prepare the body for labor and delivery, which are two very physically demanding tasks. Think of exercise as the warm-up and labor and delivery as the main events.

However, exercise during this period calls for reason and discretion. If you were playing impact sports before, you might want to consult with your obstetrician before continuing with the same. There have been instances where expecting moms who are professional athletes have been given the go-ahead to compete in their respective sports while pregnant. The decision mainly depends on your doctor's assessment of your safety and that of your baby. If you led a majorly sedentary lifestyle, your first trimester might not be the time to start training for a half-marathon.

Thirty minutes of exercise in a day, on average, is enough time for ensuring your body remains in good shape. If you led a majorly sedentary lifestyle before you got pregnant, you could start exercising by walking. Walking is always an excellent way to exercise as it is cheap and readily available. You do not need any special gear for it, and you can easily fit it in your daily schedule. It is also easy on the body as it is a low-impact exercise. It is also easy to tag along interested parties and worthy companions into a thirty-minute walk than it is for other forms of exercise.

Speaking of low-impact exercise, another option you'll need to investigate is yoga. Prenatal yoga is a safe, healthy exercise option for expecting moms that can help to reduce stress and improve sleep. Prenatal yoga also boosts the strength and flexibility of your muscles, which ultimately helps with the labor and delivery process. Prenatal yoga can also help with back pains, headaches, and even morning sickness. A thirty-minute session of prenatal yoga might be precisely what the doctor recommended. Not only does your physical well-being get a boost, but you'll also get the chance to bond with other expecting moms.

If yoga is not for you, or if you feel yoga is not enough, you can still get your recommended daily dosage of exercise through other means. Swimming, for instance, is a great way to exercise your entire body during pregnancy. Swimming comes highly recommended for expecting moms and other demographics as well, mainly because it is one of the quickest ways to boost your cardio-respiratory fitness.

Indoor stationary cycling and low-impact aerobics are other options you can investigate. Whatever you decide on, it is vital that you keep the following do's in mind:

- Wear comfortable, loose-fitting clothing, including a supportive sports bra

- Go for shoes that are designed for the type of exercise you are engaged in

- Stick to flat, level surfaces to minimize chances of injury

- Make sure to eat enough calories to meet the energy requirements of the exercise and pregnancy as a whole

- Eat at least one hour before exercising

- Keep a water bottle nearby for use before, during and after the workout

- If you need to get up during floor exercises, do so slowly to avoid feeling dizzy

As far as ensuring your well-being and that of your baby during exercise, observe the following don'ts:

- Don't engage in physical activities where falling is a possibility.

- Contact sports or activities where abdominal trauma can occur should be avoided.

- Do not participate in activities that require you to hold your breath for extended periods.

- Do not exercise in hot weather or humid temperatures.

- Do not exercise until you are exhausted; exercise during pregnancy should be done in moderation.

- Do not shock your body by engaging in intense activity after a long period of zero activity.

Before engaging in any physical activity that you fear might impact your baby, always consult with your obstetrician. It is crucial that you obtain your doctor's go ahead before getting started on any physical activity. During pregnancy, your body will change significantly. One of these changes is an increase in oxygen requirement to meet the needs of your developing baby. The increase in hormonal levels in your body will also cause your ligaments to stretch. When these ligaments that support your joints stretch, your risk of injury goes up. Lastly, you'll also experience a shift in your center of gravity because of the increase in weight and its uneven distribution. What this means is that you are more likely to lose your balance and fall over.

While you may have consulted and gotten the green light to exercise, you should still be on the lookout to determine how your body is responding. There are sure warning signs that indicate that it's time to stop exercising and speak to your doctor. These include:

- Shortness of breath
- A decrease in fetal movement
- Headaches
- Muscle weakness
- Abdominal pains
- Lightheadedness
- Vaginal bleeding
- Sudden swelling of your ankles or face and pain in your calves

Emily Green

As your pregnancy progresses, you'll probably find yourself dialing down the exercises and settling for your earlier options such as walking. This is okay and encouraged. In fact, during the last few weeks of your pregnancy, you'll want to combine some low impact exercise with lots of rest. This helps to keep the blood flowing while conserving the energy that you'll need for labor and delivery.

After delivery, it is essential to wait until your body is ready before going back to exercise. It is usually recommended that moms who have had vaginal births to wait six weeks before having a go at physical activity. If you have had a caesarian section, you'll need to wait at least eight weeks. Even though you might feel ready to jump right back to exercise immediately after delivery, it is best to wait for the recommended period to lapse. This is because while you may feel okay, your body still needs time to recover. Carrying a human being to full term for nine months is no mean feat for your body. A lot of changes will have happened within you, and your body will need to readjust to this new status minus the tiny tenant.

Labor and delivery have an impact on your physical well-being, including triggering pains such as lower back pain. Your pregnancy hormones will also linger in your body for up to six months after delivery. These hormones increase your risk of injury. As before, you'll need to discuss your plan to go back to rigorous exercise with your obstetrician.

Expecting First Time Moms

Whenever you feel ready to get started on some physical activity, start small by engaging in activities such as swimming, cycling, walking, yoga, Pilates, and even low-impact aerobics. Do not push yourself or hold yourself to extraordinarily high standards. If you are not ready to get moving, do not do it. Take your time. Even pushing the baby's stroller is enough exercise for a new mom.

Chapter 5:
Sleeping the Right Way

As you progress in your pregnancy and your bump grows bigger, you will soon realize that you will be required to make several concessions in your life. Your favorite clothes will get replaced by the more practical maternity jeans and tops, and your high heels might take a break. In their place, you might find yourself preferring less flattering footwear. Another area where you'll need to make compromises is your sleeping style. Expecting mothers need a lot of rest. This means you'll probably be sleeping a lot, sometimes even when you feel like you should not be. Increased levels of progesterone in your blood are responsible for most of the sleepiness that you'll feel, especially in the first trimester. Later, in your pregnancy, especially in the third trimester, this hormone and the exhaustion of carrying a baby will combine to keep you feeling sleepy most of the time.

There are various reasons why sleep becomes crucial when you are pregnant. First, rest is your body's downtime; a period where your body undergoes repair and maintenance. Your body will need to get enough repairs done when it's dealing with the increased demands of growing a baby. Your body is a machine, and any good machine must sometimes be shut down for repairs so that it can keep functioning well. Sleep also ensures the body is better placed to react to insulin. Your body's responsiveness to insulin is vital in keeping gestational diabetes at bay. Unfortunately for you, you might not be able to sleep as you always have. Some things will have to change.

The increased size of your abdomen and back pain are just two of the reasons why you might find yourself more uncomfortable in bed than you'd wish. Heartburn, shortness of breath, and even insomnia are others. Keep in mind that your baby will also have their own sleep schedule that might not be in line with yours. As such, while you're desperately trying to fall asleep, your baby might be keeping you awake with their nocturnal activities. During your third trimester, your baby will be big enough to deliver painful kicks and jabs. At this point, falling asleep might be harder than you thought. These are just some of the reasons why pregnant women get less sleep than their non-pregnant counterparts.

Fortunately for you, there are tips and tricks you can use to ensure that your sleep (and sanity) remains intact during your pregnancy journey. For starters, have a sleep schedule. The human body is impressive in that it can quickly adapt its clock to align to your sleeping patterns. Train yourself to wake up at the same time every day and go to bed at the same time every night. Once your body clock is attuned to this schedule, you'll find it easy to fall asleep every night. As a matter of fact, you'll see your body guiding you to sleep on those nights when you've stayed up past your bedtime. Waking up early and refreshed will allow you to have a productive day, and at the end of the day, your body will be ready to rest. This cycle is highly essential in ensuring good physical and mental health.

The second thing you should do is get enough exercise during the day. Exercising during pregnancy alleviates the symptoms of pregnancy that might make you too uncomfortable to sleep at night. These include leg cramps. Exercising also ensures that your muscles are adequately stretched, and your blood is flowing well, both of which are vital for a relaxing sleep. Stick to low-impact exercises such as walking, yoga, and swimming, and you'll have no problem falling asleep at night. A bonus of exercising is that you might be so tired that you'll have no option other than to just fall asleep.

Having a soothing nightly ritual before bed is another way to ensure that you fall asleep faster when you finally get to your bed. This ritual could be anything from a warm bath to a relaxing cup of chamomile tea or even some meditation before sleeping. Alternatively, do all three! The idea is to wind down before bed and get yourself in the right mindset for a good night of some restful sleep. There are various online resources that you can use to access guided meditation material including videos and audios which you can save to your laptop or phone for reference when necessary. You could even download sleep apps to your phone. These come with tips on how to fall asleep better and relaxing music and sounds.

Expecting First Time Moms

Limit the bed to the activities it was initially intended for, which is sleep and sex. If you are continually watching TV or using your smartphone in bed, the brain will associate the bed with those two activities. As a result, you'll always find yourself wide awake and alert when you should be sleeping. If you limit the bed to sex and sleep, the brain stores those two activities and associates the bed with them. As such, every time you get inside your bed, the mind will only be thinking of only two things. For a pregnant woman, one of those two activities will almost always carry the day.

If you are one of the women who experienced a heightened libido during pregnancy, use it to your advantage. Sexual intercourse is an excellent way to ease tension from your body and relax into a deep sleep. This relaxation can be attributed to the increased levels of oxytocin and the decreased levels of cortisol in the body. Oxytocin is a hormone that is sometimes referred to as the love hormone and is responsible for the social bonding that occurs when two people are affectionate with each other while cortisol is the stress hormone.

Making your bedroom as comfortable as possible is another way of ensuring that you sleep more easily when you are pregnant. When you are pregnant, a lot of things will make you feel uncomfortable. One of these is too much heat. Strong smells are another culprit. Whatever it is that makes you uncomfortable, ensure that it has been completely removed from your bedroom. Turn your bedroom into a sleep sanctuary. Take away everything that you don't like and replace them with the things that make you feel happy, safe, and comfortable. Turn down the heat by leaving the windows open or sleeping with a fan on. You're more likely to fall asleep when the room you are sleeping in feels like your haven.

Some women find that they are no longer able to sleep in their bedrooms, regardless of how comfortable and relaxing the bedrooms are. If this is the case, sleep where you feel most comfortable, even if it is the floor of the living area. Pregnancy is an interesting time in that you'll catch yourself having weird preferences, but the best thing to do is go along with them if they do not compromise your safety and that of the baby. If you no longer wish to sleep next to your snoring partner, change arrangements. Go with the flow and wait it out. After the pregnancy hormones stabilize, you'll find yourself returning to your normal self. At this point, you can return to your matrimonial bedroom and make amends with your beloved.

As far as sleeping positions, the best way to sleep during pregnancy is on your side. Bend your legs and knees, and then put a pillow between your legs. Better yet, sleep on your left side as this encourages the flow of blood and nutrients to the placenta and the baby. If you experience back pain while sleeping on your side, place an additional pillow under your abdomen. If you are struggling with heartburn, propping your upper body with pillows will help. You'll go through a whole lot of pillows while pregnant. A particularly handy pillow that you'll come across is the maternity pillow. Maternity or pregnancy pillows come in various sizes and shapes, but they all work similarly. They provide much-needed support and cushioning to you and your bump to ensure you are comfortable as you sleep.

You do not have to sleep in one position throughout the night; switching is fine. However, you must avoid sleeping on your back and on your stomach while pregnant. When you lie on your back while pregnant, the abdomen rests squarely on your intestines and your major blood vessels. This hinders proper circulation of oxygen and nutrients in your body and to your baby as well. The weight on your abdomen could also overwhelm your back, resulting in back pain. You might also find it hard to breathe properly while sleeping in this position. Sometimes though, you'll wake up in the middle of the night and discover that you accidentally rolled over and slept on your back just because it's what you were used to pre-pregnancy. When this happens, you should not panic. A few hours of accidentally sleeping on your back cannot harm the baby.

On the other hand, sleeping on your stomach is just plain impractical, especially when you are further along in your pregnancy. While some women can sleep face down during the early days of pregnancy, this position is soon abandoned as the bump grows more prominent. If you are very keen on sleeping with your face down, there is a pregnancy pillow that can help you do so. This pillow has been designed with consideration being given to your growing bump. It comes with a donut-like hole in the middle where your bump can rest as you snooze face down.

If you aren't getting enough sleep during the night, for whatever reason, it is crucial to schedule naps during the day. This way, you can get all the rest that your body needs. If you are unable to sleep entirely at night, do not spend hours tossing and turning in bed, as this will only lead to frustration. Instead, get out of bed, and do something relaxing that you enjoy like reading a book or having a cup of peppermint tea. Do not self-medicate with sleeping pills or any other medication while you are pregnant. This could harm your baby. You could ask your doctor to prescribe sleeping aids that are safe for you and baby.

Ensure that you take your meals at appropriate times so that they do not interfere with your sleeping schedule. Being too full just before bed can make sleep uncomfortable. Lying down on a full stomach is the perfect recipe for heartburn. On the other hand, eating several hours before bedtime might mean contending with hunger pangs when you go to bed. It is ideal to eat at least two hours before bed. If you feel hungry after that, you can take a light snack like milk and whole oatmeal cookies to sustain you throughout the night. Certain foods will keep you alert and jittery and interfere with your ability to fall asleep well. These include foods with too much sugar or caffeine content.

Expecting First Time Moms

While getting enough sleep is critical, do not set a stopwatch and demand from yourself eight or ten hours of sleep just to accomplish this goal. Watching the clock is the surest way to go crazy. Sometimes, it's best to listen to your body and just respond appropriately. If you feel energized after only six hours of sleep, then sleep for only six hours. If you are picking up the signs given by your body, you'll be fine.

Later, after the baby comes, you might find yourself not sleeping as much as you wish. Night-time feedings and a crying baby are not exactly conducive to sleeping. During the day, try as much as possible to take naps when the baby sleeps. This might be hard for the first few weeks when you feel like you have a million things to do when the baby is sleeping. However, you should be aware that you need this sleep as much as you needed it before the baby was born. Lack of sleep can make your mothering experience a dreadful one. Sleep during the day and sleep at night if you can. Alternate night-time care with your partner so that you can have reasonable amounts of sleep.

Chapter 6:
Nutrition and Top Foods to Eat

What you eat during your pregnancy will have a profound impact on you and your baby as well. As a pregnant woman, you have increased demand for calories, and you'll find yourself wanting to eat more and more. Your growing baby needs the right nutrition in terms of vitamins, minerals, and proteins to develop well. Your body also requires the right food so that it can be up to the task of growing a human being. At the same time, you want to ensure that the food you are eating allows you to lose the weight you'll have added when the baby is finally delivered. As an expecting mom, one of the best things you'll do for yourself is ensuring you eat foods that are wholesome and as natural or organic as possible. There are various categories of food that you must ensure are included in your diet so that you can meet all your dietary requirements.

Dairy Products

During pregnancy, you'll have an increased demand for calcium and protein which can be met by consuming the right dairy products. If you haven't already, stock up your fridge with dairy products, especially yogurt. Greek yogurt is an excellent bet as it contains higher calcium levels than most dairy products. Consider adding non-fat milk too to your diet and some types of cheeses such as cheddar and mozzarella. Soft cheeses are not recommended for pregnant women as they can contain listeria bacteria which can use infection. Listeria bacteria causes listeriosis which may be fatal to your unborn baby. If you are lactose-intolerant, you can still get your calcium from other alternatives including soymilk. Some people who are lactose intolerant can sometimes tolerate yogurts, especially the probiotic kind.

Eggs

Eggs are sort of the MVP of health foods, as they come with a little bit of everything. A large whole egg contains 77 calories, protein, fat, vitamins, and minerals. Eggs also provide an essential nutrient known as choline. Choline is vital for boosting metabolism and ensuring a healthy nervous system. Pregnant women who are allergic to eggs can get the choline that their bodies and babies require by replacing eggs with alternatives such as liver and turkey heart. Quinoa and amaranth also have significant amounts of choline. If you decide to go for liver, ensure that you take only small amounts of the same. This is because the liver contains very high levels of vitamin A, and too much of it can harm your baby.

Avoid eating raw eggs when pregnant as these could be contaminated with Salmonella. Foods that commonly contain raw eggs include home-made mayonnaise, lightly scrambled eggs, cake icings, and salad dressings.

Dark, Leafy Vegetables

Dark leafy vegetables contain vitamin A, vitamin K, and vitamin C. Vitamin A is an essential vitamin that ensures the proper development of the immune system and the eyes and skin. Vitamin K is critical for ensuring blood clotting in the event of injury, thus preventing excessive bleeding. On the other hand, vitamin C is an essential vitamin that has significant benefits to the human body. For a start, vitamin C is a strong oxidant that strengthens your body's immune system. Vitamin C keeps at bay high blood pressure and heart diseases and can help improve iron absorption in your body. This vitamin is also crucial in ensuring your memory remains sharp, which is a plus, especially when dealing with pregnancy brain.

Besides the vitamins, dark leafy vegetables also contain iron which is required for blood production. Iron is a key component in the production of hemoglobin which is the component of your blood that carries oxygen throughout your body. Consuming enough portions of dark leafy greens while pregnant is also a great way to get enough fiber in your body. Fiber helps with constipation, which is a problem that many women experience during pregnancy and even after delivery.

Lean Meat

Meat is a source of high-quality protein, during pregnancy and beyond. When pregnant, it is important that you stick to lean meat that has been cooked well. While you may have enjoyed a fat, juicy rare steak before pregnancy, your preferences will need to change during pregnancy. Eating fatty foods including fatty meats can harm your baby's immune system. At the same time, eating meat that is undercooked can present a considerable risk to the baby by making them susceptible to the toxoplasma parasite. The Toxoplasma parasite is a parasite that causes an infection called toxoplasmosis, which can affect the brain, lungs, eyes, heart, and liver. This infection can spread to your baby with dire consequences if not caught and treated in good time.

Whole Grains

A whole grain is any grain that comes complete in terms of containing the endosperm, germ, and bran as it came from the fields. Whole grains differ from the refined grains in that refined grains have only the endosperm. The reason why refined grains get a bad rap is that during refinement, all the critical nutritious stuff is removed and what you are left with is just starch with small amounts of protein. The important and healthy components of grains are contained in the germ and bran. This means that when you opt for whole grains, you get to eat the most useful parts which are nourishing to your body. On the other hand, binging on refined grains only helps you pile up the carbs.

Whole grains contain several vitamins including thiamin, folate, and niacin and minerals such as iron and magnesium. They also contain dietary fiber and proteins. Consuming a diet rich in whole grains can help prevent colon cancer and diabetes and reduce the risk of heart disease and Alzheimer's disease. Eating whole grains during pregnancy is a great way to set a wholesome foundation for your baby.

Some whole grains that you can look out for during your next grocery shopping trip including whole wheat, whole oats, rye, brown rice, buckwheat, quinoa, and corn.

Avocados

Avocados are one of the loveliest fruits of this planet. Not only are they so versatile in the ways they can be incorporated in a diet, but they are also packed with useful vitamins, minerals, and healthy fats. The healthy fats of avocados are useful for the development of your baby's skin, brain, and tissues. The potassium levels of avocados are also excellent in combating pregnancy cramps. You can never eat too many avocados when you're pregnant, so make sure you make that salad, have that avocado toast, go for that guacamole...the options are endless!

Legumes

There are many different types of legumes, but some of the healthiest and most common options include chickpeas, lentils, kidney beans, black beans, soybeans, peanuts, and navy beans. Legumes are a readily available and cheap source of fiber and B vitamins. B vitamins are all the vitamins found under the vitamin B complex group. They include thiamin, riboflavin, niacin, pantothenic acid, pyridoxine, biotin, folic acid, and cobalamin, which are usually indicated as vitamin B with a number suffix. These B vitamins are essential in ensuring the body's nerve and blood cells are healthy and are crucial in the formation of genetic material and DNA.

Fruits

Dried and fresh fruits should be incorporated in your pregnancy diet as often as is possible. Dried fruits such as almonds, dried apricots, cashew nuts, dates, dried figs, and raisins are an excellent source of fiber, vitamin A, iron, magnesium, vitamin E, and vitamin C, among others. The natural sugar of dried fruits is an excellent source of energy for your body while you'll need during this time. You must be careful though-dry fruits contain many calories which could lead to weight gain. Over-indulgence in dry fruits could also lead to constipation and flatulence.

Fresh fruits, on the other hand, are excellent sources of vitamin A, C, and fiber. Consider including mangoes, oranges, pears, bananas, and berries in your pregnancy diet. Fresh berries are packed with antioxidants. They are also fleshy and juicy and can help you stay hydrated.

Salmon

Pregnant women are generally advised to avoid fish that have high mercury content. Mercury is a metal that can have detrimental effects on the human body, and especially on an unborn baby. Such effects include damage of the nervous, digestive, and immune system and the kidneys as well. In instances where the levels of mercury are incredibly high, the consequences might be fatal. Fish which have been shown to contain high levels of mercury include tilefish, swordfish, king mackerel, and shark. Fortunately, salmon happens to be on the list of fish which is safe for consumption during pregnancy.

Salmon contains omega-3 fatty acids, proteins, vitamins, and docosahexaenoic acid (DHA). Omega-3 fatty acids are crucial for improved cardiovascular health while DHA is vital for the development of the baby's brain. The proteins and vitamins in salmon are beneficial when it comes to muscle growth and repair and increasing immunity.

During pregnancy, salmon should be eaten when well-cooked. You can broil, poach, or bake it. It is best to avoid raw salmon as in the case of sushi as this could place you at risk of bacterial infection. It is also necessary to ensure that you get your salmon from a trusted source.

Water

It's not really a food, but it highly ranked during your pregnancy. It is crucial that you stay hydrated throughout your pregnancy. Staying hydrated is one of the most important things you'll do during your pregnancy, and you must also ensure that your water source is trustworthy too. Water ensures that the essential nutrients are delivered to your baby, prevents UTIs and constipation, and can also help with fatigue and headaches. If you were not really a big fan of water before you were pregnant, you might want to get yourself a water bottle that you'll carry around and sip from all day.

During the first trimester, some women will find it hard to keep down even plain water. If you fall into this demographic, you might find it hard to stay hydrated. In such cases, it is necessary to investigate other alternatives including Hydrolytes Ice Blocks or poles. If the plain taste of water puts you off during pregnancy, try flavoring your water with fruit. Slices of citrus fruits like oranges and even berries are ideal. Ensure that the fruits have been washed thoroughly.

Sweet Potatoes

These two starches are ideal alternatives to wheat, as they contain good carbs and sugars that are safe for your body. Sweet potatoes are high in beta-carotene. Beta-carotene is what is converted by the body to vitamin A. vitamin A is required by the body for the proper functioning of the eyes, immune system, and reproductive systems. Sweet potatoes can be made into sweet potato flour, allowing you to bake your favorite pastries without worrying about gluten.

It can seem overwhelming at first, all these things that you are required to eat during pregnancy. It can especially be difficult in the first trimester when you must deal with nausea and morning sickness and cannot seem to keep anything down. However, you can make it easier for yourself by trying some tried and tested tips that have worked for other moms.

For a start, create a pregnancy meal plan. A meal plan is a simple way of ensuring that you always know what to eat and when. You will not have to go through the hassle of coming up with a creative new meal every day. Instead of having large meals that have been crafted to meet all your dietary requirements at once, spread your portions throughout the day. Snacking on healthy bites at intervals is a much better approach than stuffing yourself in one sitting. Small portions will also keep away nausea and heartburn.

While it has been consistently said that pregnancy is a time when you must eat for two, this is not entirely accurate. There is no pressure to overeat for the sake of overeating. Eat healthily and listen to your body. When you are full, take a break, and do something else. Your body has ways of communicating when you need to eat more, namely hunger pangs. You do not need to clear two full bowls of oatmeal for your baby to grow well. Eat well and in moderation, and especially so when you start to get those constant cravings. Giving in to all your cravings can be detrimental in the long run.

Lastly, always consult with your doctor if you are in doubt about something. There exist a lot of pregnancy-related myths online and even in social circles, and it's always best to bust them with the help of a professional.

Chapter 7:
Tips to Curb Cravings

It is common to experience food cravings during pregnancy. Thanks to all the hormones wreaking havoc in your body, you're likely to find yourself desiring the oddest foods at the oddest of hours. You're not alone. A lot of expectant mothers have found themselves in similar shoes. Typically, cravings appear at the same time as morning sickness and then wane off as the pregnancy progresses. Cravings are usually the strongest during the second trimester. Some expecting moms develop a craving for one thing that lasts throughout the pregnancy, while others will crave one thing today and a different one the next day.

For starters, it is essential to know that even science does not exactly know what causes food cravings in expectant moms! Up until this point, science has only been able to make some educated guesses. One of these guesses purports that food cravings are your body's way of ensuring you get the vitamins and minerals that you and the baby need during the pregnancy period. Another school of thought says that since you're overloaded on hormones, you might interpret smells and tastes differently. That nasty pickle that you could not stand pre-pregnancy suddenly taste like heaven. Nobody said pregnancy was going to be simple!

As a pregnant woman, it is critical to ensure that you pay attention to what your body is telling you. Craving a specific type of food might mean that your body is lacking a nutrient, which you can often get in a different kind of (healthier) food. For instance, if you find yourself craving chocolate, it's likely because you lack magnesium. You can get magnesium in bananas, dark leafy veggies, and even in nuts and grains. That is not to mean that you should never indulge your chocolate cravings occasionally. The idea here is to ensure you strike a balance between the healthy and the not-so-healthy.

There are tips that you can use to ensure that you are not overwhelmed by your cravings.

Eating more frequently is a great way to ensure that you do not confuse hunger with cravings. As an expecting mom, you'll often be hungry, sometimes even immediately after eating. During this period, your body is quickly processing whatever you take in and sending it where it's needed most. It is vital to ensure that you supply your body with what it needs when it needs it. Eat the required three meals per day, with a focus on breakfast. Breakfast is the most important meal of the day, and a good breakfast sets a good pace for the rest of the day. In between, snack healthily to ensure you are getting the nutrients that you need. Do not put in very long gaps between meals, and do not overindulge in junk food. Remember to give your body the hydration it requires by drinking lots of water after and in between your meals.

Ensuring you take a protein at every meal and snack is another tried and tested way of kicking cravings to the curb. Not only are proteins vital as they are the building blocks of life, but they also keep you feeling sated, thus ensuring you do not crave anything else. Consider adding healthy protein options such as Greek yogurt, eggs, and even nuts to your meals, paired with some healthy carbs that are low in sugar and high in fiber. This will keep away the cravings for a reasonable amount of time, after which you can snack on something else or occasionally give in to the craving.

Getting enough exercise and rest is an excellent way of managing your food cravings during pregnancy. When you are tired, your body tends to be sluggish and may function abnormally. You might end up desiring foods that are no good for you just because you are exhausted and out of it. It is critical that you exercise well and sleep well during pregnancy so that your body is in top condition. The rush and relaxation you get from exercise could very easily replace the sugar rush that you think you want.

Distract yourself from your food cravings by indulging in activities that take your mind away from food. If you're sitting idly in the house all day, you are likely to make frequent trips to the fridge. If you leave the house to walk the dog, go for yoga classes or even catch up with other expecting moms, you are likely going to forget about your cheesecake craving, even if only for an hour or two. Do not give up control over your life to your cravings.

Keep in mind that overindulging your cravings could result in a lot of weight gain, something that you might struggle with post-delivery. Sugar and junk food are two culprits that you need to be especially aware of. While you should not obsess over every pound gained during pregnancy, it is essential to be mindful of what your cravings are doing to your body. With this bigger picture in mind, you can put in place a plan to ensure you do not pack on unhealthy pounds just because you could not say no to your cravings.

Sometimes, when it comes to defeating your cravings, you'll need a partner to help you out. Put in place a plan on how to deal with your cravings, and have your partner reinforce this. Your partner could assist in various ways including portion control or even replacing the unhealthy snacks with some healthier options. Your partner could also just be that voice of reason reminding you that you can only eat so many ice-cream tubs before they become harmful to your body.

Some women will experience cravings for non-food items during pregnancy. For instance, some women will experience a strong desire to snack on items such as clay or even dirt. These types of cravings are referred to as "pica". If you strongly feel like snacking on laundry starch, do not do it. Talk to your doctor. It is likely that your body needs a nutrient, and your doctor can help you identify this and lead you towards a healthier alternative.

It is important to understand which cravings healthy and which ones are aren't. If you are craving fruits and certain veggies during pregnancy, you can happily give in to these. There is really no harm in indulging in lots of fresh fruit during pregnancy, if the fruit is properly washed. In the case of dry fruit, eating too much might cause constipation. Sometimes, cravings aren't bad at all. They can do you and your baby lots of good. On the other hand, craving soft cheeses and sushi will not have the same effect as craving fruits. This is because some foods like soft cheeses and sushi are not recommended for pregnant women as they can cause infection.

A parallel phenomenon to food cravings is food aversions. During pregnancy, you might suddenly find yourself repulsed by certain foods for no good reason at all. You might suddenly hate the smell or look of a food, even to the point of nausea. Food aversions, like food cravings, get better with time. Unless your aversion is keeping you from getting a particularly essential nutrient, it should not bother you.

Some of the foods that women commonly develop aversions to during pregnancy include garlic, eggs, onions, and even tea and coffee. If you are averse to foods that are required for the healthy development of the baby, ensure you get these nutrients in other ways. For example, if you cannot stand meat in the first trimester, make up for the deficit by eating high-protein nuts. You might also want to ensure you eat the food you hate by hiding it in something else. For example, if you cannot stand eating your vegetables, throw them in your smoothie next time you make one. This way, you'll get the nutrients you require without getting sick.

The beauty of the human body is that while some things are common for most people, everybody is different in the way it functions. As such, you might find yourself not having any cravings or food aversions during pregnancy. It is normal for a pregnant woman not to have cravings. If you are feeding well, you should not be worried about the absence of cravings. Make sure to eat healthy wholesome foods and take your vitamins and you'll be just fine.

Chapter 8:
The First Trimester, Weeks 1 to 12

The first trimester of your body announces itself in a big way. First, you'll miss your period. This is usually the first cue that you might be gaining the title of a mother in the coming nine months. Second, you are likely to deal with morning sickness, which could range from mild to terrible in terms of severity. You are also likely to be undergoing other unpleasant conditions such as flatulence. Because the first trimester is counted from week 1 to week 12, you might very well be into your first trimester by the time you find out that you are pregnant! This is because most women will usually take a pregnancy test four weeks after their last period, especially if the period is regular. If your period is irregular, you might be halfway done with the first trimester before you find out.

Lots of changes happen during this first trimester, and this is not just for the mother but the baby as well. The first trimester is when the baby goes from a fertilized egg to an embryo to a fetus. After conception, your unborn baby will be just a fertilized egg hoping to be properly implanted onto the wall of your uterus. But first things first, how do conception occur? Most people are generally aware of how conception takes place, thanks to high school biology and sex education. The magic of how your baby came to be, however, is in the details. So, what happens after ejaculation?

During ejaculation, a healthy adult male release anything between 40 million and 1.2 billion sperms. (This means that the child you are carrying is literally one in one billion). Because the vagina is an acidic environment that is not favorable to the survival of the sperm, the sperm is encased in a protective gel by the semen. Later, this gel is liquefied by enzymes that are produced by the prostate gland. This liquefaction occurs so that the sperms can be freed to travel to the eggs that are waiting to be fertilized. The freed sperms travel upwards and onwards until they get to the cervical mucus that stands guard at the entrance of the uterus.

During ovulation, the cervical mucus, which is usually acidic to keep stray sperms at bay, changes to become friendlier and more welcoming to the sperm. The mucus also acts as a reservoir where the sperms can hang out for a few days before being declared useless. This is usually for five days.

After the sperms have made it inside the uterus, they are pushed towards the fallopian tube by uterine contractions. The first sperm enters the fallopian tube minutes after ejaculation. Unfortunately, that first one is rarely the fertilizing sperm. You can think of this sperm as the recce sperm or the curtain raiser for the swimmer that will eventually carry the day.

In the meantime, the eggs that were produced during ovulation have been undergoing their journey as well. These eggs are transported from the ovary through the fallopian tube, where they await the lucky sperm. Transportation of the eggs is more graceful, with the finger-like fallopian tubes sweeping them along until they get to a junction of the tube known as ampulla isthmus. This graceful journey takes a little bit longer than that of the sperm-thirty hours to be approximate. Once the egg gets to this junction, it rests for another thirty hours. Fertilization must occur during within these thirty hours. Otherwise, the egg will no longer be viable. For the sperms that make it to the fallopian tube, it is a game of chances as far as knowing which one will fertilize the egg. The egg rests in the tube for as long as thirty hours in order to allow for full fertilization and to allow the uterus to prepare to receive the fertilized egg. After the thirty hours, the fertilized egg begins its descent to the uterus.

An egg contains a membrane that has receptors for human sperm. This membrane also plays a protective role in ensuring a fertilized egg cannot be fertilized by another sperm. This is because the membrane, scientifically known as zona pellucida, becomes impermeable post-fertilization.

You must be wondering, what about twins and triplets? Well, in the case of twins, this occurs when the fertilized egg splits into two or when two eggs are fertilized by two different sperms. In the former, the result is identical twins, while the latter case produces fraternal twins. Now, back to the baby-making class...

A fertilized egg undergoes a series of transformations before it can be called a baby. The first few days after fertilization is a period of multiple cell division, otherwise known as mitosis. The outcome of the mitosis is a mass of very organized cells that are known as a blastocyst. The blastocyst is what is implanted in the uterus, and this usually happens after it has hatched out of its protective membrane (the zona pellucida). While all this is happening, you might be completely unaware of the new life developing inside of you. However, sooner rather than later, your menses become a mystery, and you realize that indeed, you are going to be a mother.

By the time the blastocyst is implanting onto your uterine wall, you are probably four weeks along into your pregnancy. After this, you can expect your hormone levels to increase. This is because the blastocyst has hormonally signaled the ovaries to stop producing more eggs and instead produce estrogen and progesterone. These hormones ensure that you do not receive your period and boost the growth of the placenta. At week five, your baby is basically three layers, which will later form the important organs of the baby including the skin, the circulatory system, and the internal organs including lungs and intestines.

Week six marks a critical development period for your baby as it is when the spinal cord, brain, and heart develop. The eyes, ears, and upper limbs begin to make their debut, albeit slowly, and your baby starts to take on that so very familiar C-shape that you've probably seen in many fetal illustrations.

At week seven, your baby's face starts to peek from beneath the multiplying cells. The nostrils start to take shape, and so do the retinas of the eyes. Lower limbs start to form, and the upper limbs grow more pronounced.

Eight weeks into your pregnancy, your baby will have a nose. Tiny fingers will have started to form on their upper limbs, while their lower limbs will follow closely, developing into distinguishable paddles. Between weeks nine and ten, the parts of the body that have formed will become more defined. Your baby will also grow, even though its head will appear bigger than the rest of its body. At week 11, your baby's external genitalia begin to form into either a penis or clitoris. At the end of week 12, your baby has a more developed face, fingernails have started to form, and the baby weighs about 14 grams. By the end of the 12-week period, the risk of miscarriage is considered to have reduced significantly.

It is important to take great care of yourself during this first trimester as it sets a pace for the rest of your pregnancy. By the twelfth week of your pregnancy, you should have seen your doctor at least once. Your doctor will give you professional guidance on how to care for yourself during your prenatal period. They will assess your health and even that of your baby to ascertain the state of your pregnancy. If yours is a high-risk pregnancy, your doctor will discuss your options on how to best care for yourself and the fetus during this critical period.

The first trimester is a period where you might have to deal with a whole lot of morning sickness. Usually, for most women, morning sickness gets better after the first trimester. Chapter Three of this book delves deep into morning sickness and gives you tips that you can use to combat the same.

Because this is such a significant event of your life, you might find yourself feeling overwhelmed during the first trimester. Between the hormonal shifts and dealing with the shock and excitement of being a mother, it's normal to feel conflicted. It is important that you maintain a good support system for yourself during this period. Be open with your partner, family, friends, doctor and anyone else that is willing to listen. Acknowledge your feelings and emotions, talk about them and work through them. It might seem very confusing at the start, but things tend to get better as you move along the trimesters.

Chapter 9:
The Second Trimester, Weeks 13 to 26

Most expecting moms are happy to get into the second trimester of their pregnancy, as it tends to be the most comfortable of the three. During this second trimester, you'll most likely have overcome the uncomfortable signs of pregnancy including morning sickness. Your appetite will most likely be back, and your energy levels will be looking good. Some expecting moms will also experience an increased sex drive during this trimester. Most of your clothes will still fit in the second trimester. This is the one trimester where you can make the most of your pregnancy before the exhaustion and discomfort of the last trimester kicks in.

Your baby will also be making the most of this trimester as well. In the second trimester, your baby makes great strides in terms of their development. At the end of your first trimester, your baby will be about four inches long and weighing in at an ounce. You can expect this to go to twelve inches and two pounds at the end of the second trimester. Quite some impressive growth! What this means for you is that you'll also be steadily gaining weight as you consume enough food to make up for baby's demands. The steady weight gain of the second trimester should not concern you if you are eating healthily. Once the baby is out, you can quickly shed off the extra pounds through exercise.

So, what exactly happens to your baby during this second trimester period? Your baby's limbs which started developing in the first trimester are usually well defined by the time you hit the second trimester. Their genitalia are also fully developed, and you can now schedule an ultrasound to check your baby's gender. Your baby is also starting to become their own person-they can yawn, make faces, and later, they'll start making good use of their little legs and arms by throwing some most adorable jabs and kicks.

Your baby's hair will start to grow at week 16, and by week 22, they'll have a decent amount of hair, including eyelashes and eyebrows. Because the baby's digestive system was fully formed by the end of the first trimester, the second trimester is all about putting it to practice. Your baby will now start practicing for life outside of your womb by sucking and swallowing. They can even taste the food you eat at this point, so make sure you snack on the healthy stuff if you are hoping to influence his preferences.

The second trimester marks a period of refinement and re-organization for your unborn, with most of the organs developed during the first trimester being fine-tuned. For instance, the ears and eyes will be moved to their correct positions during the second trimester. The brain will start to control their heartbeat-which has previously beaten spontaneously-and their eyelids as well, allowing them to blink. In short, your baby will be starting to function like a little normal human being.

What to Do During the Second Trimester

As an expecting mom, there are several things you can do during the second trimester to ensure that you are entirely in control of your pregnancy as is humanly possible. One of the things you need to investigate is amniocentesis. At week 15 of the second trimester, consider scheduling multiple marker tests to check for any chromosomal abnormalities. The window of opportunity for the testing of these abnormalities is typically between weeks 15 and 20. It is vital that you get your unborn baby screened so that you are prepared for what to expect. In the case of severe abnormalities, your doctor will discuss your options with you.

Another thing you'll want to decide is whether you want to find out the gender of your baby. Some parents are excited to find out, while others like to keep it as a surprise until delivery time. Whatever the case, the second trimester affords you the luxury of choice as far as the gender reveal is concerned. By this time, your family and friends already know you're expecting as you'll likely to have announced after the first trimester. Even the ones you haven't told yet will be able to make out a noticeable baby bump. The choice to check your baby's gender should be yours to make and not brought on by the pressure of an impending baby shower or gender reveal party.

While you haven't started feeling physical discomfort during the early second trimester days, you can bet it is coming. Invest in comfortable sleepwear during your second trimester. This could be anything from some comfy pajamas to a body pillow. If your mattress or bed isn't comfortable enough, consider changing to a better alternative. You'll be glad you did this while your bump was still reasonably sized. Later, as your baby grows and you progress to the second trimester, mobility might be a challenge. So, get comfortable now. Store the nuts for the winter while you can still move them, so to speak.

Second-trimester preparations will also include signing up for a childbirth education class, either alone or preferably with a partner. Such courses fill up quickly so the faster you can get into one, the better. Besides childbirth classes, don't forget to also engage in activities that you enjoy. Yoga, Pilates, walking, reading books, napping, and staying hydrated are essential. Do not neglect the little events that you enjoy. With your child-free days quickly coming to an end, it is imperative that you relish this alone time while you can.

The second trimester is an ideal time to get started on decorating the baby's nursery. If you already know whether you are getting a boy or girl, you can paint the nursery in hues and tones that will appeal to them. Even if you've chosen to keep the gender a surprise, you can still tastefully decorate the nursery in neutral colors. Alternatively, go for the road less traveled and go for whatever colors you prefer, traditional gender stereotypes aside. Whatever it is that you choose, make good use of the energy levels of the second trimester. A time will come in the final trimester when all you want to do is nap all day, and you will not do the nursery any justice then.

Besides getting the baby screened, you'll also want to be tested as well. If you have a medical history of it or are at risk, get checked for gestational diabetes. Your doctor will do this by scheduling a glucose screen, which usually happens between weeks 24 and 28.

Other things to consider during the second trimester include narrowing down on the baby name options, going for one last trip or babymoon, and arranging for post-maternity leave childcare if you are planning to resume work.

At the end of week 26 of the second trimester, you'll likely find yourself feeling more discomfort that you did at the beginning of the trimester. Hormonal fluctuations, swelling, and headaches might become the norm. Prioritize your well-being in terms of exercise, staying hydrated, and eating healthily, and consult with your doctor in case you are worried about something. You might also start to experience another pregnancy phenomenon-the Braxton Hicks contraction.

Emily Green

Braxton Hicks contractions are the body's way of preparing for labor. You'll know you are experiencing them when your abdomen or groin areas tighten and then relax. These contractions can be mild or strong, and even though they begin as early as seven weeks, you'll not likely feel them until later-maybe 16 weeks or so. Braxton Hicks contractions are sometimes referred to as "false labor". If your Braxton Hicks is making you uncomfortable, try lying down or going for a walk, depending on what you were doing before they started. Taking a relaxing bath or a massage can also help.

As your pregnancy progresses, false labor can be very concerning, especially to a first-time mom. Call your doctor if you are worried about the contractions you are experiencing. You should especially call your doctor immediately if the contractions are followed by vaginal bleeding, leaking of fluid, and noticeable change in baby's movements and/or severe discomfort that you cannot "walk off". If you experience continuous contractions that come five minutes apart in an hour, call your doctor or midwife immediately.

Chapter 10:
The Third Trimester, Weeks 27 to 40

The third trimester of your pregnancy journey starts at the end of week 27 or the beginning of week 28 and lasts until you give birth. This could be up until week 40 or even later. Some women have been known to have a delay of up to 42 weeks or more. This is to be expected and should not be cause for worry unless your doctor says otherwise. Some babies require just a little more time, while others are ready to make their debut on their exact due date.

During this last trimester, you will probably be moving slower or even less, and you'll be wondering if you could possibly get any bigger. The answer is yes! Your baby is not done growing, and in the coming weeks, you'll feel and look bigger. As the third trimester ends, your baby will be approximately 50cm long and at 7.5 pounds will weigh as much as a small pumpkin.

Your baby transforms quite a bit during this last trimester. For starters, their cartilage changes to bones. This is your cue to ensure that you keep consuming as much calcium as you can to ensure the proper development of your baby's bones. Foods that contain calcium include dairy products such as milk and yogurt, and dark, leafy greens as well. Oranges are also a source of calcium. Instead of opting for store-bought orange juice, go for organic oranges in all their farm glory. If you find it hard to eat oranges, make your own orange juice at home using a blender or juicer.

The other thing that will be changing in your baby is the skin. Throughout the first and second trimester, your baby will have a translucent skin through which you can see their organs. In the third trimester, your baby's skin becomes opaque. They will also start to accumulate fat under their skin as they prepare for their debut in the big world. As a result of these changes, the vernix, and lanugo that have previously protected your baby will start to shed, their way of taking a back seat as new protectors come into place.

It will likely please you to know that your baby's five senses are fully developed around week 30 of pregnancy. Now is your chance to sing to the baby, introduce the baby to your loved ones, and even play with a flashlight shone over your belly. Your baby will now have a sense of what is happening in the outside world, and you'll probably notice them react when your partner starts talking to you. As your baby grows and becomes more alert, you'll notice the kicks and punches becoming more powerful and, in some instances, painful. This is set to continue until the last weeks of pregnancy when the movements become more subdued as the baby grows bigger and starts running out of space.

The third trimester is also a period of significant development for your baby's brain. During this trimester, your baby's brain starts to test some skills including blinking, regulation of body temperature, and dreaming. It can be surprising too many to learn that unborn babies dream. After all, what experiences do they have to dream of? It is a fact however that unborn babies and newborns dream of what they are familiar with and that is the sensations that exist in the womb.

Your baby's first poop starts to build up in the baby's intestines in the final weeks of pregnancy. This poop is referred to as meconium and is a mix of blood cells, lanugo, and vernix. Your baby will take this first poo a day or two after they are born. In some instances, the baby will poo in the womb. When this happens, an emergency C-section is usually recommended to ensure that the baby's airways are not blocked by the meconium. Meconium staining is just one of the several causes of fetal distress. Other causes of fetal distress (when baby's oxygen supply is compromised) include placental abruption, umbilical cord compression, and maternal illness. Placental abruption is said to have occurred when the placenta separates from the uterine wall during pregnancy. This separation is dangerous as it means the baby is unable to receive the oxygen delivered by the placenta via the umbilical cord.

As the third trimester nears to an end, your baby will drop lower in your pelvis in readiness for being born. This phenomenon is known as lightening and can occur two to four weeks before delivery in first-time moms. Dropping does not necessarily mean that you're about to go into labor anytime soon. At your antenatal appointment, your doctor will check how far the baby has dropped. In some instances, the baby might drop with its feet or bottom instead of its head. When this happens, the baby is said to be in breech position.

A baby in breech can be handled in several ways. One of them is to deliver the baby as it is with the buttocks or feet coming out first. Breech births are not a favorite of most doctors and moms as they can compromise the well-being of the baby. This is because easing the baby's head from the birth canal becomes harder when it's the last thing that delivered. As the baby's legs and bottom are delivered, the cord can easily wrap around the baby's neck thus cutting off oxygen. This risk posed to the baby is the main reason that most doctors will recommend either turning the baby and getting it settled in the headfirst position or going for a C-section.

While your baby readies herself for the outside world, your body will also be undergoing a variety of changes. For starters, on a very general level, you'll be feeling very uncomfortable. You'll find it hard to move as fast as you used to, you might feel big and bloated, and you'll be making even more frequent trips to the bathroom than you used to. As your bump grows to accommodate your growing baby, you might start to experience cramps or sharp pain around the abdominal area as the ligaments stretch. There is not much you can do about these pains besides lying down and taking it easy when they happen.

Besides feeling uncomfortable, you'll also feel exhausted during your last trimester. Pregnancy is a highly demanding task on a human body, and nine months of it is no joke. To deal with fatigue, eat well, get some exercise, and get enough rest. While you might feel like it's a ridiculous suggestion to exercise when you feel so tired, it is for the benefit of your body that you keep moving. Exercise releases endorphins which can make you feel more positive and energized. Staying active also helps your body get ready for the very physical activity that is delivery.

Heartburn is another problem that is commonly experienced by pregnant women during the third trimester. As your bump gets bigger and bigger, your uterus tends to push your stomach and its contents upwards leading to heartburn. Heartburn can be highly uncomfortable and painful. The milder cases of heartburn can be treated at home using tested methods such as eating small meals several times per day instead of one large one and using over the counter antacids. Severe cases of heartburn should be attended to by a doctor, who may recommend other options such as prescription H2 blockers. H2 blockers are medicines that are used to treat conditions related to excess stomach acid. Sitting upright and standing are known ways of maximizing space in your abdomen. Whenever you can, avoid lying down too much and especially after eating.

Emily Green

False labor, otherwise known as Braxton-Hicks contractions, can be very concerning during the third trimester. Your baby is big enough to survive in the outside world and any sign of labor, true or false, can send a first-time mom running to the delivery room. During the third trimester, Braxton-Hicks contractions will make a somewhat regular appearance in your day to day life. As you near delivery, it is important to have familiarized yourself with the signs of true labor. True labor occurs in contractions that have regular intervals, that usually become stronger as time progresses. True labor cannot be quietened with movement, which is typically the case for Braxton-Hicks. True labor comes with back pain and usually some vaginal discharge. You may also notice the passage of the mucus plug that blocks the cervical opening. If you are experiencing true labor, get in touch with your doctor. If you are experiencing false labor (which is the opposite of true labor), go for a walk or lie down.

While in your third trimester, you should start putting the final touches to your delivery plans. One of the things you'll need to do is investigate your maternity benefits and apply for maternity leave if you have not already. Maternity leave can be taken anytime from at least four weeks before delivery, although this might be subject to your specific region's employment and labor laws and your employer's policies.

The third trimester is also an appropriate time to decide what kind of birth you prefer if you have not already. Some women prefer to give birth in a hospital while others would much rather go for home births. Some prefer vaginal birth and yet others are all for C-sections. While these conversations are best had earlier when you have enough time to consider all options, you can still decide in the third trimester. However, the longer it takes you to choose, the fewer your options will be. For instance, a home birth requires that you have a trusted midwife and doula to help you deliver your child. It is essential that you identify a midwife and doula earlier on in the pregnancy so that you can cultivate a respectful and comfortable relationship over the nine months.

If you are resuming work after delivery, finalize on your childcare options. Childcare options could range from hiring a nanny, finding a suitable daycare, or even enlisting the help of a family member. Make sure that you tie all the loose ends of childcare before the newborn comes along. It can be overwhelming planning things while taking care of a newborn who hasn't let you sleep in two weeks!

A lot of women experience a nesting urge during these last weeks of pregnancy. Nesting is the urge to clean things and organize them properly. As the due date nears, you might find yourself getting worked up over the state of the house or the nursery. There is really no scientific reason why the nesting urge affects some pregnant women. There are only good guesses as to why this might be the case. Anticipating the arrival of this brand-new family member can excite a soon-to-be mom enough to want to clean everything and everywhere. Sometimes, nesting can also be brought on by the fact that logically you know you will not have enough time to clean after the baby comes. You might feel an overwhelming urge to clean everything before the baby arrives because you know that logically you have more time to do so before the delivery.

If you are delivering at the hospital, the last weeks of the third trimester are an excellent time to pack a hospital bag for yourself and the baby. A hospital bag contains all the essentials that you will require for delivery and those that the baby will need after birth. These essential items include the hospital paperwork including your ID and insurance cards, bathrobe, socks, your essential oils, baby's clothes, a collection of your favorite relaxation music, your birth plan, and even your favorite pillow. When packing for the hospital, ensure you take into consideration what you'll require during the delivery and after. Some moms tend to pack for the labor and delivery, and the baby, and forget that they'll need some things for when the baby has already arrived. A more comprehensive list of what to include in your hospital bag can be found in Chapter 15 of this book.

Chapter 11:
The Stages of Labor

For a first-time mom, labor can be both an exciting and frightening experience. You've probably heard less-than-pleasant labor stories from friends, family, and even strangers online and are worried about your own experience. A good thing to remember is that every labor experience is different; no two births are identical. Even for you, if you decide to have multiple children, every subsequent delivery will vary from the previous. There are four stages of labor that every woman will undergo during childbirth.

First Stage of Labor: Early and Active Labor

The first stage of labor is commonly the most prolonged of the four stages and can last anything from a couple of hours to several days. This time tends to be shorter for subsequent deliveries. The first stage of labor is usually divided into two phases, namely early and active labor. Early labor is the onset of true labor pains, which involve the dilation of the cervix in preparation for the baby's debut into the birth canal. Besides dilating, your cervix will also soften and become thinner, a process referred to as effacement. While this is taking place, you'll feel mild irregular contractions. You might even notice a clear or pink vaginal discharge. This discharge is caused by the disintegration of the mucus plug that forms at the cervical opening during pregnancy.

Most women go through early labor comfortably, with little to no pain. Your normal activities need not stop while in early labor, as you wait for the contractions to grow in frequency and intensity. For first time moms, it is natural to panic when true labor kicks in. There's no cause for alarm though, and you should only head to the hospital when the contractions become intense, if you're bleeding vaginally, or if your water breaks. The best way to stay calm during this stage is to get in touch with your doctor for updates and keep your labor support partner close.

You can also go for a walk, take a bath, or listen to relaxing music to keep calm and relaxed during early labor. Because of how unpredictable early labor is in terms of duration, you might be indulging in your bath, walk, or book for a long or very short while before you get into active labor.

Active labor is the phase of the first stage of labor where your cervix dilates wide enough to accommodate passage of a baby. Active labor is where the real work begins. When you are expecting, your cervix is usually about 3cm in length. When active labor sets in, your cervix will dilate to 10cm, up from the 6cm it dilated during early labor. Active labor involves more discomfort and stronger contractions. Most women experience leg cramps, nausea, and even pressure on their back. Active labor should ideally find you in hospital. If you haven't already gotten to the delivery facility by the time active labor kicks in, do so immediately. You'll need the medical experts by your side when going through active labor.

Typically, active labor lasts about eight hours, with your cervix dilating 1cm everyone hour. Some women are lucky to have shorter active labor periods. Try and remember everything you learned during the childbirth classes to ease your discomfort during active labor. If you require pain medication, ask for it. You are best suited to decide your pain threshold, and your doctor will be on hand to discuss your relief options with you. Taking a walk, getting a massage, and breathing between contractions will help you feel better during this phase. You could also have a warm bath and roll on a birthing ball.

The last fifteen to sixty minutes of active labor are referred to as the transition. During this phase, your contractions are very intense and close together. This is perhaps the most painful stage of labor, and you'll need all the support you can get. Expect to feel some pressure on your back and rectum areas, and at times an overwhelming urge to push. If you are not dilated enough, your obstetrician will advise you against pushing. This is because you might get too tired and cause your cervix to swell before the baby is ready to be delivered.

Second Stage of Labor: Delivery of the Baby

The second stage of labor follows closely behind the transition stage and is the stage when you deliver your baby. This stage calls for you to channel all the calories you indulged in during your cravings and push with all you might. For some lucky moms, the second stage of labor lasts only a few minutes. For others, this stage can last several hours. First-time moms tend to take longer to go through the second stage.

During this second stage, your doctor will instruct you on when to push and when to take a break. It is recommended that you take a breather between contractions. As a first-time mom, it is essential to determine what works best for you so you can push efficiently and effectively. Some moms will prefer to push while squatting; others will do it while on their hands and knees. Choose a position that works well for you and change this whenever possible, so you do not cramp up in one spot.

If you are wondering how pushing happens, think of it as having the most massive bowel movement of your life. This might sound gross, but it is the most accurate analogy. While the pain of the contractions might be overwhelming at this point, try your best to relax your body, and focus on the push. Release the tension from your face and shoulders and concentrate on getting that baby through the birth canal. Some moms will experience an overwhelming urge to push, and this is normal. Push as much as you need to, but don't be frantic about it.

Expecting First Time Moms

When you feel a contraction building up, take a deep breath so that you can be prepared to push through it. If your obstetrician instructs you to stop pushing, pay attention and do as told. Sometimes, the doctor will ask you to take a break so that you can regain your energy. They could also do so to prevent the baby's head from being pushed out too quickly.

While you push and hope for the baby to be born quickly, the delivery team will be ensuring that they're ready for the baby's debut. They'll do this by arranging sterile drapes and instruments and donning their surgical scrubs and gloves. The delivery team will also monitor the baby's heartbeat throughout the labor period using a fetal monitor and give you the support that you need to deliver successfully. The fetal heartbeat is monitored so that the baby can be checked for distress as things can also get difficult for the baby during delivery.

After you've been in active labor and pushing for a while, a phenomenon known as birth crowning will occur. Birth crowning is the gradual emergence of your baby's head through your vaginal opening. Crowning signals impending birth and the period between crowning and delivery can be as short as ten minutes or less. If you need some motivation, you can touch your baby's head when it crowns or use a mirror to take a good look. Sometimes, all a pushing mom needs is some physical evidence of the gift awaiting them at the end of those contractions.

After birth crowning, your baby's head will finally emerge from your birth canal, followed by the rest of the body. If your baby is stuck in your birth canal, your doctor can manually deliver the baby using forceps or other means. Once the baby's head and shoulders are delivered, your doctor or midwife will most likely suction their nose and mouth to get rid of amniotic fluid. Further suctioning may be done after the entire baby is delivered if your doctor deems this necessary. Suctioning helps to ensure that the baby does not inhale the fluid into their lungs.

After your baby is outside of your womb, it is essential to keep him or her warm as they are not able to immediately regulate their temperature. The doctor or midwife will place your baby on your abdomen to keep him warm and to help you bond. It is normal to be too tired to properly bond with your baby at this point. If this is the case, your birth partner can step in to ensure the baby gets some skin-to-skin warmth and bonding.

The baby's umbilical cord will also be clamped in two places, and a cut will be made between the two points. If your partner is present, they can do the honor of cutting the umbilical cord. The baby does not feel any pain while the cord is being cut since the cord does not contain any nerves. The reason why it does not contain any nerves is that it is not actually made of skin or connective tissue. Instead, the umbilical cord is formed from what is known as Wharton's jelly. Some doctors recommend waiting a few minutes before cutting the umbilical cord. This is to ensure that enough blood flows from the placenta to the baby, thus lowering the risk of newborn anemia. After the umbilical cord is cut, blood will be collected from it to determine the baby's blood type. This blood may be used for other tests as well.

One to five minutes after your baby is born, the medical team will carry out an assessment known as the Apgar assessment and give your baby an Apgar score. The Apgar score indicates your baby's readiness to meet the world without medical assistance. The evaluation will measure the baby's muscle tone, heart rate, breathing, and response to reflexes. If your baby scores well on the Apgar assessment, you will be able to keep him with you. If not, the medical team might take him away for further checks. When all this has been done, you'll be ready to proceed to the next stage of labor and delivery, which involves the delivery of the placenta.

Third Stage of Labor: Delivery of the Placenta

After the baby is born, you're likely to focus all your attention on the miracle lying softly in your arms and forget all else. But not so fast, you need to deliver the placenta as well. The placenta is a very useful reservoir for nutrients and oxygen that has been helping to nourish your baby in the womb. Now that your baby is out, this reservoir needs to come out too. After the delivery of your baby, your contractions will not cease immediately. You will continue to experience close but less painful contractions, and these will help you deliver the placenta. Placenta delivery typically takes five to ten minutes. Some women might take longer.

Your doctor will check to see if the placenta is intact after it is delivered. If it is not intact, the placenta remnants in your womb must be entirely removed to ensure you do not get an infection.

Fourth Stage of Labor: Recovery

The final stage of labor and delivery is the recovery. This starts right after you're done delivering the placenta and continues months after you go home. After nurturing an entire human being in your body, and pushing it out to the world, your body is not quite what it used to be. It is vital to ensure that it returns to its natural state for your continued well-being.

One of the things your midwife or doctor will do to kick-start the recovery process is to massage your uterus. Massaging your uterus is a technique used to prevent uterine atony which causes post-partum hemorrhage, a leading cause of maternal deaths worldwide. Uterine atony is a condition whereby the muscles of the uterus fail to contract after birth. A uterine massage contracts your uterus back to its standard size and contracts the blood vessels that were previously feeding the placenta. Besides the uterine massage, your doctor might also stitch you up if you experienced tears or had an episiotomy during delivery.

Expecting First Time Moms

Your doctor will also check your vitals, which include your heart rate and blood pressure and if everything looks good, you'll probably only need some rest before you can start receiving visitors. Some moms will also experience intense hunger after delivery. With all the calories you'll burn during labor, you can indulge in your favorite meal soon after birth. Many moms claim that the first meal you have post-delivery will taste like the most delicious meal of all time even if it is just a simple peanut butter and jelly sandwich!

Two to three days of observation in a hospital are all you require if you've had a vaginal birth with no complications. If you have had a C-section, you might need to stay in the hospital longer so that the doctors can monitor your recovery from surgery. C-Section moms usually go home after three to five days, depending on each situation. After the two or however many days you need in the hospital, your doctor will give you the okay to head back home with the newest family member.

You'll need to take it easy once you get home. Eat lots of healthy foods, drink plenty of fluids, and get enough rest. The first few weeks post-delivery can be intense, and it's okay to feel overwhelmed physically and even mentally. Always reach out and ask for help whenever you need it and accept it when it is freely offered. For the first few days, focus on ensuring you and the baby are well-taken care of. Other tasks like doing the laundry and dusting all the corners of the house can be outsourced to a willing family member or housekeeper.

Chapter 12:
Hypnobirthing

Ask any woman, even those who are not moms, and they'll tell you that labor and delivery are a harrowing experience. This is because pain is what women have been conditioned to expect. In films and television shows, labor is depicted as this horrific event, with the mom-to-be screaming her lungs out and a dedicated medical team instructing her to push as hard as she can. In female conversations about childbirth, there is almost an unwritten rule that the most horrendous labor story gets the prize. Granted, labor is not exactly a walk in the park. It also doesn't have to be a screaming fest of intense and excruciating pain. A woman can deliver her baby in an experience that makes them feel calm and in control. Hypnobirthing is the practice that seeks to give expecting mothers control over their childbirth experience, ensuring more relaxed and less painful labor.

If you walk into a delivery room armed with horror stories of childbirth, you'll be tense and fearful. This fear is counterproductive because it causes you to have an increased level of adrenaline in your body. Adrenaline interferes with the release of oxytocin, a hormone that is needed to progress labor along. When the production of oxytocin is affected, your labor will be longer. Hypnobirthing equips you with techniques for ensuring that you stay calm and allow the necessary hormones to flow naturally, thus ensuring your labor is not prolonged more than is necessary. Hypnobirthing teaches women that they can give over their bodies to the magic of birthing while maintaining control over their minds.

So, what exactly is hypnobirthing and how did it come about? Hypnobirthing is a term that is derived from the word hypnosis and birthing. Even though it includes the word hypnosis, you should not expect anyone to hypnotize you in the traditional sense of the word. There will be no swinging watches in the labor room seeking to send you to the other realm. The hypnosis that occurs during hypnobirthing is majorly self-hypnosis and would perhaps be more aptly named as meditative labor. You will be hypnotizing your mind so that it can positively endure the process of giving birth. Hypnobirthing focuses on three main techniques which are controlled breathing, meditation, and visualization.

The origins of hypnobirthing can be traced back to a British obstetrician named Dr. Grantly Dick-Read who came up with what is called the FTP theory. FTP theory stands for Feat, Tension, and Pain. In his approach, Dr. Dick-Read stated that fear causes tension which, in turn, causes pain. This pioneering doctor further argued that fear during childbirth causes blood to be diverted away from the uterus, which starves the womb of the oxygen it needs to deliver the baby.

When this happens, the uterus does not function as intended, and labor becomes a prolonged and painful experience. Dr. Dick-Read ended his theory on the note that 95% of labor pains are caused by fear and tension, and women would benefit from less painful labor by incorporating relaxation techniques in their childbirth process. While Dr. Dick-Read pioneered this theory, it was not until later that the term hypnobirthing came to be. Michelle Leclaire O'Neill coined this term in 1987 in the USA. O'Neill is a published author of many books on childbirth and is an expert on hypnobirthing and pregnancy.

Most childbirth classes teach expecting moms how to breathe during labor, but very few go into the meditation and visualization practiced in hypnobirthing. The next sections of this chapter explore in depth the concepts of controlled breathing, meditation, and visualization that every mom expecting to have an almost painless birth should be aware of.

Controlled Breathing

When a first-time mom who is afraid of childbirth goes into labor, the last thing they are thinking of is how to breathe calmly. Yet, this is precisely what they need to ensure that their labor and delivery is as enjoyable as is humanly possible. During fear and panic, breathing is a labored process. You're likely to be taking puffs and gasps which will do nothing for your body and the baby that is about to be born. Learning how to control your breathing, especially during labor, will give you back control over the pain you expect to feel when giving birth.

Controlled breathing is used as a relaxation technique in that it sends signals to the brain. These signals, in turn, let your brain know that you are not under any stress and no stress hormones should be released. Stress hormones can interfere with the release of hormones that are needed to progress labor. Controlled breathing usually focuses on the speed and depth of breath. Deciding whether to breathe through the mouth or nose is another way of practicing-controlled breathing.

During labor, it is advised that you breathe in deeply through your nose and exhale through your mouth. While exhaling, focus on releasing all the tension that has built up within your body. Tension and stress make it harder for the baby to come out because it tightens the muscles. At the early stages of labor, breathing is usually slow. Later, it might become lightly accelerated and progress to even faster paces when you are about to deliver. The idea is to have you as the expecting mom in control of how you are breathing, regardless of whether that's slow or fast so that you can 'breath the baby down' instead of pushing endlessly amidst screams and pain.

Meditation

In a world that is fraught with ups and downs, unpredictability, disaster, and worries, choosing to focus on the positive is an art.

Meditation is a technique that involves focusing your mind in a way that achieves calmness and relaxation. Meditation requires you to tune out the distractions happening around you and focus on achieving maximum mental peacefulness. For pregnant moms, this is a skill that is very handy. Luckily for you, you can learn meditation and practice until you get better, in time for your delivery.

The first step to meditation in hypnobirthing is to get into a comfortable position. If you are uncomfortable and dealing with aches and pains, your mind will be distracted, and you'll not be able to meditate properly. Put on some relaxation music and start the process of settling your thoughts. Start by focusing on the positive outcomes of the delivery and replace any feelings of fear with thoughts of positivity. Think of how beautiful and loved your baby will be. Take deep slow breaths and remind yourself that you'll soon be a mother to be a most incredible baby.

Practice meditation throughout your pregnancy so that you know what works best for you by the time you go into labor. Enlist the help of your partner so that you have a sidekick in your meditation journey. Your partner can also help you in other ways such as putting together a CD of your favorite relaxation music. When you positively prepare your mind for the task ahead, you'll find it easier to go through labor.

Visualization

Expecting First Time Moms

Delivery rooms are not the fanciest of places and walking into one can be somewhat scary. Thankfully, you can imagine yourself in a different place if the delivery room is not doing it for you. Remove your mind from the present and think of how wonderful it will feel to have your baby in your arms. If you have a favorite place that you like to go, think of yourself as being there. If you need a trusted pillow or lip balm to help you visualize better, carry it with you to the hospital. Thinking of things that make you feel happier will help you labor more peacefully, which is something that every woman can appreciate.

A combination of controlled breathing, meditation, and visualization can make a huge difference when it comes to delivering your first child. Getting mentally ready for your baby is as important as preparing physically.

A hypnobirthing course is typically covered in five classes, which are two-hours long on average. You may begin attending classes at any time between weeks 25 and 30. Some women attend classes right until the very last week. This can be impractical for some, especially when you take into consideration time and cost commitments and the physical exhaustion of the third trimester. You can supplement classes with books and online tutorials, especially if you are constrained for time or money, or both. When it comes to hypnobirthing, you'll need a birth partner to attend it with you. Some childbirth classes feature only the moms. Hypnobirthing is different as the birth partners have significant roles in ensuring the techniques learned are put to good use.

In hypnobirthing, the birth partner lightly massages the mom in labor while reminding the mom of what they need to be doing. Many classes usually provide a handbook with all the phrases and techniques that the birth partner needs to remember during birth. You are also likely to get a hypnobirthing CD that you can play on repeat during birth.

Taking control over the birth process using hypnobirthing helps to reduce the trauma associated with childbirth. It is unfortunate that a lot of mothers are scarred for life by the experiences they undergo in the labor room. Fortunately, with hypnobirthing, you can ensure that you do not suffer nightmares after delivering your baby. Hypnobirthing does not promise to deliver zero pain, but it does promise to lessen the pain and make your childbirth memorable in a good way. Some quick tips to remember about hypnobirthing are:

- Hypnobirthing is recommended for first-time moms and moms who have delivered before

- Hypnobirthing can be learned as a home study course or by attending classes

- You can still receive medical intervention should you need it

- Hypnobirthing can be incorporated in any birthing plan

- Even if your doctor or midwife does not understand hypnobirthing, you can discuss your choices with them and get their support

- You can go through hypnobirthing on your own if you do not have a partner

Myths About Hypnobirthing That Are Not True

Unfortunately, as it is with most things, there exist several myths about hypnobirthing that confuse first-time moms and moms looking to give hypnobirthing a go. One of the most common myths is that hypnobirthing will cause you to be so out of it that you'll not even be aware of what is happening in the delivery room. This is incorrect. The idea of hypnobirthing is to get the mom in such a relaxed state that external stimuli do not bother her. It does not mean relinquishing control over to someone else. It means acknowledging that you're in charge and controlling the outcome of your labor.

Another common myth is that hypnobirthing makes labor so pleasurable that you'll want to get another child immediately. Hypnobirthing is not about eliminating pain; it's about preparing the body and mind to endure whatever pain comes your way. It is impossible to have a labor that is completely painless. Even if you take medication, pain is a very subjective and relative matter.

Lastly, there are certain pockets of people who believe that hypnobirthing is a woo-woo type of theory that is practiced by people who also encourage free-range parenting and other new-age theories. This could not be further from the truth. Hypnobirthing is premised on scientific facts regarding how the body reacts to various stimuli such as fear, and there are real benefits to be gained from opting for hypnobirthing.

Chapter 13:
Post-partum Recovery

As an expecting first-time mom, you've probably gone through multiple books, blogs, videos, and even classes on what to expect during pregnancy and childbirth. It is natural to want to be unprepared. Unfortunately, a whole lot of the resources available to pregnant women focus on just that: pregnancy and childbirth. As such, lots of moms find themselves surprised when it comes to dealing with life after childbirth, and specifically, post-partum recovery. This chapter will focus on the surprises to expect after delivery and tips that you can use to recuperate faster and better after bringing your baby into the world.

After delivery, your doctor will advise you on how long you'll likely take to recuperate. Typically, if you have had a vaginal birth, it is estimated that you'll require six weeks to heal. For caesarian section moms, this period is usually 12 weeks. While this period estimate is given in good faith and based on historical data and years of medical research, you must keep in mind that bodies heal differently.

During pregnancy, many women gain weight thanks to all the eating and snacking they do to keep up with their increased demand for calories. Right after delivery, a lot of women find themselves worried about this extra weight and what to do with it. The first week after delivery will see you shed some pounds when the retained fluids exit your body. However, for the pounds brought on by the fact that you gained during pregnancy, you'll need a different strategy. For many women, this strategy involves exercise. If you were reasonably active before you got pregnant and during your pregnancy, you can easily resume exercise a few days after childbirth especially if this was a vaginal delivery. However, you will need to ensure that this exercise is light and friendly to your body which has undergone a significant event. Always check with your doctor before getting started on any exercise.

Keeping an eye on your diet is another way of ensuring you lose the extra pounds and stop more from piling. A healthy diet will also ensure your body gets the nutrition it requires to heal and produce milk for your new baby should you choose to breastfeed. As a bonus, breastfeeding your baby is another great way of losing weight. This is because breastfeeding makes use of the fat cells stored in your body during pregnancy.

Besides weight gain, your libido is another issue you might have to deal with after delivering your baby. It is a common occurrence for new moms to lose their sex drive to the extent where they have zero desire to be intimate with their partners. There are several reasons for this. For starters, being a mom to a newborn is not exactly a walk in the park. You're likely to feel exhausted and even overwhelmed, especially when your new bundle of joy decides to cry all night. While in this state of fatigue, you are not likely to be thinking of bedroom antics with your partner.

Your new body image is another factor that can contribute significantly to a decreased sex drive. When pregnant, your body will change to include things that were not previously present. You might develop stretch marks, your tummy will no longer be as taut as it was before, and you'll likely add weight in places you'd rather not. Some women take a while to accept this new body, and this affects their self-confidence. A woman with a negative perception of their body is unlikely to want to strip naked and be intimate with their partner. If you are going through the struggle of accepting your new body, it is important to share your fears with your partner.

A good and supportive partner will reassure you and help you come up with ways to feel better about your body. For instance, you could sign up for exercise classes together. You could also try other ways of being physically close such as taking baths together. What's most important to remember though is that this is your new body because you are in a new phase of your life. You're a different woman, one with the esteemed title of mom. You cannot quite go back to your young, single, and child-free body because that is no longer you. The journey to self-acceptance after childbirth might take a while, but it is highly recommended that you get started on it.

If you are breastfeeding, you might experience a decreased sex drive due to a decrease in levels of estrogen in your body. When this happens, you might experience vaginal dryness which will make sexual relations unpleasant. If this is the case, consider using lubricant during intercourse. If your libido doesn't get any better after several months, you might want to see a doctor.

Post-Partum Depression

Post-partum depression, also known as post-natal depression, is a form of mood disorder that comes about after childbirth. PPD can affect both genders but is usually most common in new moms. This depression manifests itself in various ways including extreme sadness, low energy levels, crying episodes, irritability, and even changes in sleep and eating patterns. The unfortunate thing about PPD is that it can easily go unnoticed, leaving new moms suffering in silence. Unfortunately, this silence has ended fatally for some moms.

Scientists have pointed fingers at several things as the reasons why post-partum depression occurs in new mothers. One of these is the sudden and significant decline in hormones post-delivery. During pregnancy, the female reproductive hormones increase tenfold. After childbirth, these hormones -estrogen and progesterone- drop back to their pre-conception levels. These hormonal fluctuations can negatively affect a new mother, who, at the same time, is dealing with the exhaustion of taking care of a newborn. At the same time, new mothers also must undergo the psychological re-alignment of taking care of this new person who is totally dependent on them for their survival. When this happens, especially in the absence of a support system, a new mother can easily sink into post-partum depression.

Some groups of women are at a higher risk of suffering from post-partum depression than others. If you have a history of depression, you are more likely to suffer PPD. Younger mothers and mothers who were ambivalent about their pregnancies are also high-risk candidates for post-partum depression. Your home situation is another risk factor that could put you at a higher risk of developing post-partum depression. For instance, if you are living alone with limited social support or if you are undergoing marital conflict, you are likely to find yourself battling with depression after delivering your baby.

Post-partum depression is usually hard to self-diagnose because some of its symptoms mimic the usual baby blues that a woman undergoes after delivery. Baby blues are the mood swings that women go through during the period after delivery. These are majorly caused by the hormonal changes and the adjustment to motherhood. Baby blues are a somewhat mild form of post-partum depression and typically go away after two weeks.

If your baby blues persist beyond these two weeks and last well over a few minutes every day, you might be suffering from post-partum depression. If this is the case, you'll need to see a doctor who can recommend medication and counseling. Consider seeing a doctor if you persistently experience the following symptoms and signs after delivery:

- Excessive fatigue that doesn't seem to go away
- Difficulty sleeping even after trying all recommended remedies
- Feelings of worthlessness
- Suicidal thoughts
- Homicidal thoughts or thoughts of hurting someone else
- Feelings of hopelessness
- General lack of interest in life
- Loss of appetite
- Loss of libido that doesn't improve after a few months

Post-Partum Psychosis

Post-partum psychosis (PP) is a form of severe mental illness that some women suffer after delivery. This form of psychosis can happen out of the blue to women who do not have a history of mental illness.

Expecting First Time Moms

Women who have PP experience hallucinations and can easily harm themselves and other people. For this reason, post-partum psychosis is almost always treated with medication and hospitalization. The good news is that PP can be treated, and the mother can easily resume their mothering role in their child's life.

Post-partum depression can easily go undetected as the mother can easily fake a smile when expecting guests or when hosting family and friends. However, post-partum psychosis easily announces itself. There will be delusions, paranoia, confusion, and a general shift in the person's normal behavior. As a new mom, you might not be aware that you have PP as you will have lost touch with reality. It is crucial that you accept the help offered to you by family and medical professionals during your post-natal period as most of it is well-meant. If you do not feel much like yourself after childbirth, be open to discussions on how you can get better.

Generally, whether you are afflicted by the blues or not after delivery, there are several things that you can do to ensure you recover well after childbirth. For the first few weeks after your delivery, find a way of relieving yourself of all your duties other than feeding your baby and taking care of yourself. The few days and weeks after delivery are not the best time to be hauling large loads of laundry or spring cleaning the house. Ask for help from your friends, family, and even partner. Hire a housekeeper if you can afford to. A time will come when you'll be able to do the heavy lifting and that time is not right after you deliver.

It is critical for new mothers to learn how to stand up for themselves. This means not having to apologize for your preferences and parenting style. If you wish to breastfeed or bottle feed your baby, do so without apologies. If you need to take a nap while friends and family are visiting the new baby, proceed with your nap unapologetically. As miraculous as parenting is, it also opens a whole new realm of critics who are ready to dissect all your moves. Responding to each critic is the surest way to feel drained.

Find a support group of new and experienced moms to draw strength from. You might be comforted to know that little Jess isn't sleeping through the night either. There's always something you can learn from other mothers that will make your motherhood journey easier. This is especially true down the line when you need some of those tried and tested home remedies for dealing with colicky babies and teething problems. Do not isolate yourself while on the motherhood express.

Forgive yourself for the unrealistic expectations you had set for yourself before you had the baby and set new realistic goals. If you had previously thought you'd go back to size zero after only a few weeks only to find yourself having added more weight, forgive yourself, and start walking. Incorporate your baby in your exercise by taking along their stroller during your evening walks. Be easy on yourself if you have ordered takeout dinner more days than you made a home meal. You're a new mother with a new baby, and things will take time before they are "perfect".

Keep in mind all the physical problems that you might experience post-delivery and seek help on how to manage them. Women who have given birth are likely to experience constipation, incontinence, hemorrhoids, and sore breasts. Constipation after delivery can be caused by several factors. If you have a C-section, constipation could be brought on by the fact that you underwent major surgery and the digestive system needs time to recover. Pain relievers administered during labor can also slow down the digestive tract. A sore perineum can also scare a new mother from making a bowel movement if they fear tearing their episiotomy stitches. Whether your constipation is caused by physiological or psychological factors, you can relieve the problem by eating high-fiber foods coupled with drinking plenty of water. Do not ignore the urge to do as holding back only makes the stool harder which makes it more painful to pass.

Urinary incontinence after birth is common, especially in women who have delivered vaginally. Urinary incontinence happens when the muscles and ligaments that support the urethra are stretched during labor and delivery, thus easily allowing urine to leak out. Urinary incontinence usually resolves within a year of delivery. Kegel exercises and lifestyle changes can help you regain control of your bladder. In severe cases of incontinence, there might be a need for medical intervention including electrical stimulation therapy and surgery.

Returning to work after birth is another topic that first-time moms should pay attention to as they consider their post-partum recovery. Your first day back at work might be wrought with anxiety, worry, restlessness, and even depression. Some employers are very supportive of returning moms, while others aren't. If your employer falls in the latter category, make sure of the benefits offered to returning moms to make your transition easier. Flexible working hours, for instance, come in handy when a mom needs to feed their baby first before reporting to work. If your employer is not keen to make allowances for you, make sure you have a solid child-care plan back home. Alternatively, consider changing employers and going for a job that supports the social development of their employees. Whatever decision you make, keep in mind that you are protected by the employment and labor laws of the region you work in.

Chapter 14:
Detrimental Mistakes to Avoid During Pregnancy

So, you're pregnant with your first child and wholesomely excited about this journey. You're also terrified because well-meaning friends and family have laid bare all the gruesome details of pregnancies, labor, and delivery. To get prepared for your bundle of joy and your new role as a mother, you have read all the pregnancy books you could lay your hands on. You still do not feel ready. You fear that one wrong move will end up in disaster. While you had initially planned on enjoying your pregnancy to the fullest, you are finding yourself battling nerves and anxiety continually. What to do?

This chapter outlines the top mistakes that you should avoid during pregnancy. Once you have these committed to memory, avoiding them should be easy. You can after that look forward to enjoying the incredible journey that is bringing a human being into this world.

Indulging in Alcohol
Most expecting moms know that they are not supposed to indulge in alcohol while pregnant. What some moms do not know is that there are plenty of products that have alcoholic content that you might be

using unknowingly. Such products include mouthwash, flavored extracts, nail polish remover, aftershave, perfume, and even some bug sprays. To avoid inadvertently interacting with alcohol, always read the ingredients label of the product that you purchase. After having your baby, avoid indulging in too much alcohol especially if you are breastfeeding.

Too Much Coffee

While you might like your cup of coffee, you'll need to cut back on the caffeine once you find out that you are expecting. Doctors recommend reducing the daily intake of caffeine to 200 milligrams, which is what you'll find in a regular cup of coffee. Caffeine can also be found in black and green tea, so you'll need to watch out for those as well. During the first few months of pregnancy, caffeine can make your morning sickness even worse. It is yet another reason why you need to go slow on the caffeine.

Type of Food and Portions

While you may be 'eating for two', it is important that you ensure you are eating the right food and the right portions. Eating everything in sight, junk food included, is not the proper way to go about your pregnancy diet. While you might feel the need to indulge your cravings, ensure that you are keeping a healthy balance between what is needed by the baby and what you need. Discussing your diet options with your doctor is a great way to approach your food habits during this period. Also, if it's fatty, spicy, raw, or questionable, forego it until after the baby is born.

Attitude Towards Pregnancy

There are several things about you and your life that will change when you become pregnant. You might have to avoid certain foods, increase your vitamins intake, and maybe say goodbye to contact sports for a while. You should not treat pregnancy as a condition or sickness. While you need to be more careful, it does not mean that your life must come to an end. Pregnant women can, and should, carry on with their lives as they have done before. You should still be able to go to work, engage in your hobbies, go for that shopping spree, cook your favorite meals, and hang out with your friends as you have done before. At the same time, you should remember that the rules that applied before you were pregnant still apply. If it wasn't a good idea before you were expecting, it still is not a good idea after finding out you are pregnant.

Avoiding sex

Some women will experience a heightened sex drive when they are pregnant. On the other hand, some women will completely wipe out sex from their schedule. Unless your doctor warns you against sexual activity, it is necessary to continue being intimate with your partner. Sex during pregnancy has excellent benefits which include improved blood circulation. It also increases bonding with your partner and boosts your self-confidence. In the later stages of pregnancy, sex can help induce labor. This is because the prostaglandins contained in the semen can soften the cervix and pelvic muscles and aid in contractions. If you start to feel uncomfortable during sex as the bump grows, switch positions and find one that works best for you. Stay open and honest so that your partner is on board with ensuring your comfort comes first.

Lack of Sleep

Even though you have a busy lifestyle with a million things to do, it is essential to get enough sleep. Getting enough rest ensures that your body gets the rest it needs to recuperate from all the heavy lifting of growing a human being. It is recommended that pregnant women get at least ten hours of sleep every night. Some pregnant women will completely neglect rest, which is detrimental both to you and your developing baby. If you're having trouble sleeping, refer to Chapter 5: Sleeping the Right Way for tips and tricks on how to make bedtime easier for you and your growing bump. Remember that you do not have to sleep only at night. You can reduce your sleep deficit by stealing small naps during the day.

Too Many Vitamins and Supplements

You might be feeling excited about getting all the necessary vitamins and supplements for your baby, but don't overdo it. Your baby's primary source of nutrition should ideally be the whole, healthy foods that you consume. The vitamins and supplements are intended to supplement your everyday diet and not replace it. Don't avoid vitamins, but don't depend on them either. If in doubt regarding where to draw the line, consult with your doctor. If you have been taking prenatal vitamins before you got pregnant, consult with your doctor so that you know whether you should keep taking them. Too much of anything is harmful, and this applies to prenatal vitamins also. Your doctor might recommend taking specific vitamins and supplements for only a few months of the pregnancy. This is fine as they'll usually have a good reason for recommending this.

Too Much Sun

Sunbathing is fantastic and all but not so much when you are pregnant. Expecting moms tend to have more sensitive skins. As such, you should take great precaution to avoid the dangerous effects of too much exposure to direct sunlight. Wear enough sunscreen for protection, stay in the shade, and drink enough water for hydration. Too much sun can cause heatstroke which is terrible for the baby. Overheating is the same reason why some schools of thought tell moms not to soak in hot baths for an extended period. Your baby can regulate their temperature only after they are born and not immediately so. While they are in the womb, your baby depends on you to make wise decisions about when to bask in the sun and when to stay in the shade. If you experience overheating while in the house or outside going about your work, try sucking on an ice lolly or placing a cold compress behind your neck.

Socializing with Sick People

While you might love your aunty dearly, you might also want to wait until she overcomes her nasty chickenpox before hugging her too tightly. Pregnancy is a sensitive period, and your immune system is usually running at less than optimum ability. Do yourself a favor and avoid sick people to avoid getting sick yourself. Even if you have obtained the necessary vaccines, exercise discretion and caution. Speaking of vaccines, you'll probably want to read up on the vaccines that are necessary for expecting moms and newborns. Staying informed will help you make informed choices for your baby and for yourself too.

Stressing Over Everything

In life, even the best-laid plans come with flaws and deviations. Things will most definitely not always go according to plan when you're pregnant either. While pregnant, you're hormonal and emotional, and it can be easy to get carried away by everyday stresses. Do not make the mistake of being so caught in the hassles of life that you forget to enjoy the journey you are undertaking and the miracle that you are creating. When you start to feel overwhelmed, stop and exhale. Stop and ask for help. Stop and have some chamomile tea. Stop and nap. It is highly advisable that you remain aware of your breaking points and ensure you do not get there. If you have experienced depression in the past or any other mental illness, talk to your doctor so that you know what help is available for you.

Obsessing Over Your Image

You're pregnant. Your body is literally manufacturing a human being inside of you. Most people do not expect you to look like a Victoria Secret's model during this period of your life. Embrace the way your body is changing without feeling ashamed of it. A lot of pregnant women make the mistake of hiding their blossoming bump under layers and layers of frumpy clothing. Do not fall into the trap of demanding perfection from yourself just because you have been fed the same by media outlets and the likes. While pregnant, you are only required to stay healthy, take care of yourself, and feel good about yourself. Your stretch marks should be worn loud and proud. Get some nice well-fitting clothes and enjoy all the thrills and frills of maternity fashion. You deserve it.

Making the Announcement Too Soon

After finding out that you are pregnant, allow yourself and your partner to digest the information before sharing it with everyone else. Walk around with the knowledge that your love has brought forth a new person, without inviting anyone else to share the secret. There is really no pressure to share this information with everyone else, and especially not your friends and followers on social media. And when you are genuinely comfortable sharing this information, you can make your grand announcement from the rooftops. Typically, couples will wait until eight weeks before announcing because then the risk of miscarriage is expected to have reduced. Still, no rule says you cannot wait longer.

Being Crippled by Your Fears

It is normal and natural to have great fears during pregnancy, especially when not-so-nice circumstances are surrounding you. If you have experienced miscarriage before, it is natural to fear the same happening again. If you have tried to conceive for the longest time before finally falling pregnant, it is normal to feel apprehensive about the pregnancy. If you are going through pregnancy alone, it is entirely human to feel scared out of your wits. Do not let the fear overcome you. There has been a lot of stigmas associated with matters of pregnancy in the past. Things are getting better now, and there are a lot more people willing to listen. Find one of those and open. Pregnancy is an extraordinary journey, and you should never allow your fears to stop you from enjoying it. And remember, just because you do not feel like it does not mean you'll not be a badass, kick-ass momma. You've got this figured out way more than you think you do. Whatever you haven't figured out, you've got the rest of your life (or at least eighteen years) to do so!

Too Much Planning or Not Enough Planning

You can plan the perfect birth plan for the entire nine months of your pregnancy and still be caught flat-footed on the day of the delivery. The best way to ensure you enjoy your pregnancy, through to labor and delivery, is to prepare for the essentials without obsessing over details. Your baby will not necessarily dance to the tunes outlined in your birth plan, and you can bet something will go wrong somewhere.

Instead of playing out the perfect birth over and over in your mind, prepare your mind and body for the honor of giving birth. Exercise, eat well and meditate. Take childbirth classes that teach you the practicality of giving birth.

On the other hand, winging it during pregnancy will just not cut it. Even if you are not keen on planning, iron out the necessary details of labor and delivery before you go into the delivery room. Choose a doctor you trust, get your insurance in order, enlist the help of a birth partner, prepare yourself mentally, and prepare the nursery for your baby's homecoming. Even having a rough plan is better than not having a plan at all.

Not Attending Childbirth Classes

Childbirth classes are a useful tool to make use of during a first-time pregnancy because they teach you things nobody else has taught you before. While mothers and daughters tend to discuss a whole lot of things, it's unlikely that your mom has taught you how to breathe correctly during labor. It is important to be confident in your ability to deliver without someone needing to give a PowerPoint presentation of how it's done. On the same note, it is important to appreciate that as a first-time mom, there are a lot of things you do now know yet. Childbirth classes teach you these things so that you are aware of what to expect and what to do when things do not go as expected.

Playing Doctor

Pregnancy is not a time to self-medicate. Just because a certain page on the Internet said you're suffering from a disease doesn't mean you should rush and buy the medicine. Never self-medicate during pregnancy. Always consult with your doctor. Some medicines that were safe for you before pregnancy could have detrimental effects on your unborn baby. If you are dealing with aches and pains, ask a doctor to recommend a safe painkiller that you'll use throughout the pregnancy. Alternatively, consider relieving your pains in other ways instead of rushing for a pill. For example, instead of treating your headache with pain relievers, try addressing the root cause of the headache. This could be dehydration or even stress. Drink enough water and take it easy, and you are likely to suffer fewer headaches.

Keeping the Wrong Company

That friend that encourages you to drink while pregnant and doesn't believe in the dangers of smoking is not a good friend to keep around when pregnant. Your friend from work who tells you it's okay to stay up partying all night while you are six-months pregnant is lying. You will be required to stay conscious of who in your circle means well for you and who doesn't. After your baby arrives, this will be even more important as you do not want them to grow up in a toxic environment. Sometimes, in some very unfortunate circumstances, this means keeping a distance from your baby's father until you are ready to deal with them in an empowered manner. Life is not easy, and it

Expecting First Time Moms

doesn't get easier during pregnancy. However, you are not powerless, and you can control some things in your life.

Chapter 15:
Top Pregnancy Tips and Essentials

Pregnancy is a beautiful adventure that is experienced by a woman, their partner, and loved ones, and the miracle they are carrying within them. While all pregnancies involve the conception and development of a human being within the loving and haven that is a womb, every woman experience pregnancy differently. Certain things have been tried and tested and found to be true for most pregnancies. In this final chapter, you'll find top pregnancy tips and essentials that will come in handy during your nine-month rollercoaster.

Maternity Fashion

At some point in your pregnancy, your go-to jeans stop being your go-to jeans. The lovely dress that you wore at every occasion takes a back seat, and all your nice tops seem like a joke now. This is because your bump has grown, and nothing fits anymore. During the entire first trimester and part of the second trimester, you can get away with sticking with your pre-pregnancy wardrobe. However, at around the seventh month, you'll have to change to a more pregnancy-friendly wardrobe. Maternity jeans, leggings and maternity bras are just some of the essentials that you need to have. Maternity bras are especially important in ensuring your breasts stay supported during this period when they are becoming fuller and heavier. When choosing maternity bras, do not go for bras with underwire. Underwired bras can squeeze the breasts awkwardly, and make you feel uncomfortable. The last thing you need is something to inhibit the comfort of your breasts which are now fuller and tender in readiness for nursing. Remember that maternity fashion does not need to be boring. You can have fun with colors and prints. Whenever possible, go for items of clothing that you can wear even after you deliver your baby. When all is said and done, the best maternity fashion is whatever makes you feel comfortable and good about yourself.

Childbirth Classes

As a first-time mom, you'll need all the information you can get about pregnancy and childbirth. Hopefully, this book has answered most if not all the questions that you have about pregnancy and childbirth. Consider supplementing the information in this book with some practical childbirth classes. There are different types of childbirth education classes including Lamaze classes, Bradley Method classes, and Hypnobirthing classes. The Bradley Method classes teach that childbirth is a task that female bodies were designed for and that, with the right preparation, women can go through birth without suffering. Lamaze classes teach women to trust their intuition during childbirth and empowers them to make informed decisions about their healthcare, when pregnant and beyond. Childbirth classes can be attended on your own or with your birth partner. It is ideal to have your birth partner with you so that they can use the skills and techniques learned in class to support you during childbirth.

Essential Oils

During your pregnancy, essential oils are going to come in handy in several ways. At the onset of your pregnancy, you are likely to experience lots of morning sickness. Lavender, peppermint, ginger, and chamomile will help you feel a whole lot better. These essential oils can make you feel better even when you're not pregnant! Pour a drop of any of these oils on a cotton ball and sniff away. Alternatively, just inhale directly from the bottom. You could also leave open bottles of essential oils strategically placed in your bedroom or living room area so you can inhale the essence all day.

As your pregnancy progresses, especially in the third trimester, you'll find that your vaginal and perineal area might become irritated and puffy. You might end up feeling uncomfortable and even itchy. To prevent this from happening, use cypress, geranium, and lavender to soothe this area. Just pour a drop of each in the palm of your hand and mix together and then apply to your lady parts. An alternative to the coconut oil is olive oil. Taking care of your southern bits during pregnancy will help them recover well from the exertion that is childbirth.

Essential oils also come in handy when it comes to helping you fall asleep better. Pregnancy comes with many surprises, and one of those might be difficulty falling asleep. Chamomile and lavender are exceptionally useful in helping you fall asleep during those nights when insomnia kicks in. Some calming essential oils can also be used during the process of labor to relax the mom-to-be. These oils should be used in collaboration with the relaxation techniques learned during childbirth classes.

Mental Health

The changes, both physical and physiological, that take place in your body can overwhelm your mind during pregnancy. It is critical that you remain aware of the state of your mental health during pregnancy. It is common for women to experience depression and anxiety during pregnancy. For women who have a history of mental illness, discontinuing intake of medication for the sake of the baby can have a detrimental effect on the mom's well-being. Keep the lines of communication with your doctor open during pregnancy so that they can jump in and assist for instance by recommending a therapist when needed. If you are lucky enough to have one, make use of your support system. Meditate. Go for yoga. Take long walks and breaks when you need them. Nobody said that you must achieve everything in one day. Pregnancy is a nine-month journey, but a whole lot of it is taking each day as it comes.

Constipation

Constipation affects a lot of women during pregnancy. Constipation can lead to swollen hemorrhoids, which tend to be very painful. Swollen hemorrhoids develop in the anal area when a lot of pressure is applied to the area, which is typical when you are struggling to have a bowel movement. The best way to deal with constipation is to avoid it before it happens. Immediately after finding out that you that you are pregnant, ensure your diet is high in fiber and stay hydrated by drinking enough water. Whole grains and dark leafy vegetables are examples of foods that are high in fiber content.

If you've had a C-section, the pain that comes with making a bowel movement can put you off from going to the toilet when you need it. Put aside this fear and power through your bowel movement because if you don't, you'll get constipated, which is even more painful. Contact your doctor if your constipation is coupled with rectal bleeding as this might indicate a bigger problem.

Intimacy

After your baby is born, you might not have the time or energy to spend a whole lot of romantic time with your partner. The pregnancy period is your last chance to enjoy some alone time with your partner without worrying about the baby. Some women tend to shy away from sexual intimacy during pregnancy since they're worried about how they look or because they feel uncomfortable. Some are even worried that sex might hurt the baby. Your baby is well protected in the uterus by the amniotic sac and will not be bothered by a little lovemaking.

Unless your doctor advises otherwise, it is safe to continue being intimate with your partner. Intimacy can also be spending time without getting physical. After the kids, it becomes harder to be spontaneous. Make the best of the pregnancy period to schedule intimate and spontaneous getaways with your man.

Memories

You will only ever be pregnant with your first baby once, so make sure you take enough photos to last you a lifetime. Immortalize your pregnancy journey by hiring a good photographer who will give you professional shots that you'll be proud of. If you are not up to hiring someone, just take the photos yourself. Thankfully, you only need a smartphone with a high-resolution camera to take all the photos that you want. Pictures are great for looking back on and even sharing with the baby once they're old enough to appreciate what you went through to bring them to this earth.

Prenatal Vitamins

Prenatal vitamins are taken to help cover the nutritional gaps that exist in the diet of a mom-to-be. They do not help you get pregnant, but they help the body to be ready to nurture a baby once you become pregnant. Prenatal vitamins supply the body with vitamins and minerals such as the B vitamins, vitamin D, iron, folic acid, and even calcium. It is best to start taking prenatal vitamins at least three months before conception. Women who do not intend to get pregnant should not take prenatal vitamins as prolonged use could lead to accumulation to toxic levels.

Vaccinations

Over the years, vaccines have become a controversial topic with some groups of thought informally referred to as "anti-vaxxers" campaigning vehemently against vaccinations. As a first-time mom, it is essential to get all the information first before making a decision that could potentially harm your child and even put their life at risk. At a fundamental level, it is essential to understand how a vaccine works. A vaccine is administered to stimulate the immune system so that the body can develop defenses to attack a pathogen should that pathogen manifest in the body later.

Vaccines are used to prevent certain diseases. The intended end goal for vaccines is to achieve herd immunity and eliminate certain diseases. So far, only smallpox has been eradicated through vaccination. It is hoped that other diseases such as polio and measles can soon follow suit. While pregnant, you'll receive some vaccines to protect yourself and especially the baby. After the baby is born, they will require vaccines too. Common vaccines administered to babies after birth include the chickenpox vaccines, hepatitis, measles, and meningitis.

Hospital Bag

Expecting First Time Moms

A hospital bag is a bag, suitcase, or trunk-full of items that you carry with you when going to the hospital to give birth. You should pack your hospital bag when you are 37 or 38 weeks pregnant, or earlier if you anticipate labor to begin before your due date. The items that you pack in your hospital bag can make all the difference between having a comfortable stay in the hospital and having an awful one. Usually, the items that you'll pack are what is required for the birth and what is needed after birth. Make a checklist of all the items that you require to make sure you do not forget to pack anything. Some things that you'll need to include in your hospital bag are:

- Mandatory documents such as insurance and identification cards

- Comfortable wear that you're okay staining, including socks, a warm sweater or robe, and clothes for going home

- Phone and charger for you and your partner so you can keep family updated

- Relaxation material such as your favorite music or magazines to pass the time with

- A receiving blanket for baby and other warm blankets for the ride home

- A warm set of clothes for baby; your partner or a trusted friend can bring more sets during visits

- Travel-size toiletries including shampoo, lotion, toothpaste, deodorant, and a hairbrush for you and your partner because it gets sweaty, and you'll need to clean up

- Eyeglasses or contact lenses if you wear them to see your bundle of joy when they are finally delivered

- A nightgown that you can easily say goodbye to when it gets ruined

- Maternity underwear if you do not want to wear the hospital-issued underwear

- Your favorite pillow so that you can get as comfortable as you possibly can during labor

- A breastfeeding pillow so that you can comfortably breastfeed your baby after they arrive

- An infant seat for the journey home; if you forget this, you will not be allowed to take the baby home

- A change of clothes for your partner who has been working so hard to cheer you through labor

- A camera and charger, if possible, with back-up power and memory, to capture all the important moments

Breastfeeding

It is usually recommended that breastfeeding should begin immediately after birth or as soon as the baby and mom are stable. Newborns are typically able to latch onto a breast immediately after birth, although some require some pushing. When a newborn is placed in their mother's arms, they instinctively start to seek the breast. This is because they learned how to suckle while still in the womb, often practicing on their own thumbs, and are ready to get started on the real thing.

For the first few moments when you start breastfeeding, you might experience soreness in your nipples which can be very painful. You might even experience cracked or bleeding nipples, a condition which can be excruciating and even put you off breastfeeding. Usually, it's okay to keep breastfeeding your baby even if your nipples are cracked or bleeding. There are some measures you can take to alleviate the pain. One of them is applying a moisturizing cream or cold compress and using hydrogel pads to soothe your sore nipples.

It is common for a breastfeeding mom's breasts to become engorged when they are full of milk. When this happens, you might feel a lot of pain which is only relieved when the baby feeds or some of the milk is let out of the breast. As a first-time mom, it is necessary to be aware of the difference between normal engorgement caused by too much milk and mastitis, which is a more severe and painful condition. Mastitis occurs when bacteria enters the breast or when a milk duct becomes blocked. Signs of mastitis include breast pain and swelling, fever, and red blotches on your skin. Your breasts might also feel hot to the touch, and you might notice some lumps. If you suspect you have mastitis, get in touch with your doctor. This condition is usually solved with antibiotics in the case of a bacterial infection and usually resolves within a few days. In severe cases, there might be a need for incision and drainage.

While breastfeeding is a great way to provide nourishment to your child while bonding with them, consider introducing a bottle later so that your partner can relieve you of night feeding duties. Training your baby to use a bottle will also come in handy when you resume work as someone else can feed them while you are away. Exclusively bottle-feeding your baby is fine too and has no bearing on the sort of person they will become once they grow up. With bottle-feeding, you'll need to ensure that the bottles are properly cleaned and kept sterile so that your baby is not at risk of falling ill.

Home Birth Vs. Hospital Birth
As an expecting mom, you can choose to give birth at a hospital or in your home. Pregnant women prefer to give birth at home for various reasons, a top one being that the familiar surroundings of home can be relaxing during labor. If your doctor or midwife gives the okay, you

can comfortably give birth at home, surrounded by family if you so wish. Home births are usually less costly than hospital birth and tend to be devoid of the pressure to use medications. They are also more convenient as you do not need to travel to the hospital when labor begins. You'll tend to feel more comfortable giving birth at home, especially if you fear hospitals. You can also indulge in your religious or cultural practices much better at home as this is your safe space. On the flipside, home births tend to be messy. You might also require urgent medical intervention, which will mean being rushed to the hospital in the middle of labor.

A hospital birth, on the other hand, is statistically safer and should be the only option for women with high-risk pregnancies. You will also have a larger medical team at your disposal when you give birth in a hospital. Even at a hospital, your views are listened to. If you do not want pain medication, nobody will force it down your throat. You should not be discouraged from giving birth in a hospital just because you are fearful.

Embarrassing Moments of Childbirth

You may have heard it before and cringed inwardly, but it is true-it is normal to have a bowel movement during childbirth. This information is probably the last thing a first-time mom wants to hear. Just thinking of going number two while everyone peeks at your nether regions is enough to make you swear off childbirth for the rest of your life. The good news is that your medical team will have experienced these numerous times before and will most likely keep experiencing it after you've delivered and gone home. Your doctors and nurses are prepared for the messes of childbirth, and you can bet nobody will bat an eyelid when your bowels refuse to cooperate.

Hopefully, your confidence as a first-time mom-to-be is higher now than it was when you started reading this book. It is normal for new moms to experience angst about pregnancy and motherhood. A few months with your baby are all you will need to realize that you are well-suited for this honorable role, regardless of how you might feel on some days. Keep in mind too that billions of women have walked this journey that you are about to walk and successfully so. You, like the rest of them, will be just fine.

If you find this book helpful in anyway a review to support my endeavors is much appreciated.

Expecting First Time Moms

Emily Green

www.ingramcontent.com/pod-product-compliance
Lightning Source LLC
Chambersburg PA
CBHW060453080526
44584CB00015B/1422